January

THERE'S A WHOLE YEAR OF EXCITING EVENTS AHEAD. LET'S GET STARTED, DON'T BE LATE!

Universal
Letter-Writing Week
(second week)

Oatmeal
Month

National School
Nurse Day
(4th Wednesday)

UNIVERSITY OF NV LAS VEGAS
CURRICULUM MATERIALS LIBRARY
101 EDUCATION BLDG
LAS VEGAS, NV 89154

What Happened Today? • EMC 1015

Happy New Year! The first recorded bowling match took place on this day in 1863.

▶ The game of bowling has many words with multiple meanings. What are the many definitions of the following words?

    bowl   strike

    spare   pin

▶ Name all the other games you can think of that are played with balls.

▶ Find out how bowling is scored.

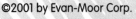

In 1974, U.S. President Richard Nixon reduced the speed limit on highways to 55 miles per hour. The new speed limit was meant to conserve energy consumption.

▶ What does limit mean? What is consumption?

▶ Why is it necessary to obey the speed limit?

▶ What are the current speed limits on highways and freeways in your area?

In 1888 wax paper drinking straws were patented by Marvin Stone. Mr. Stone believed that people would enjoy drinking lemonade through straws. He created paraffin-coated straws that were small enough that lemon seeds wouldn't fit through them.

▶ The word straw has several different meanings. Think of as many as you can. Give a sentence for each different meaning.

▶ List all the different inventions that have been created to help people eat.

▶ Choose one of the inventions you named. Find out who the inventor was and when the item was invented.

Louis Braille was born in 1809. Louis was blinded by a bad accident when he was three years old. He wanted to develop an alphabet for blind people. An army captain told him about a dot-dash code punched in cardboard called night writing. Mr. Braille used this idea and created a writing system for the blind that uses raised dots.

▶ What does the word blind mean?

▶ Can you identify the five senses? If you had to be without one sense, which one would you choose? Why? How would your life change?

▶ Find a copy of the Braille alphabet. What would your name look like if it were written using this alphabet?

Dancer/choreographer Alvin Ailey was born in 1931. He decided to study dance after seeing a dance performance on a junior high field trip. His style combines modern dance, ballet, and jazz.

▶ How would you explain what the word dance means? What does a choreographer do?

▶ How many different types of dances can you name?

▶ Find out more about Alvin Ailey.

Sherlock Holmes, the famous fictional detective, was "born" in 1854. Created by Sir Arthur Conan Doyle, a Scottish optician, Mr. Holmes was a chemist, a violinist, a swordsman, and the main character in sixty stories.

▶ What is a mystery? What does the word fictional mean? Give a synonym and an antonym for fictional.

▶ Has anything mysterious ever happened to you? Tell about it.

▶ Find a mystery story and read it.

The first American bank opened in Philadelphia in 1782.

▶ Can you explain the multiple meanings of these words
bank   vault   safe
deposit   interest

▶ Besides a bank, where else do people keep money?

▶ Do a survey. Find out where your family and friends keep their money. Create a graph showing the results of your survey.

Today is Rock and Roll Day in honor of Elvis Presley's birthday. He was born in 1935.

▶ The words rock and roll have multiple meanings. How many different meanings can you give for each word? Write a sentence using each meaning.

▶ Name different kinds of music. Which one is your favorite? Why?

▶ Find the titles of as many of the songs that Elvis Presley recorded as you can.

In 1788 Connecticut became the fifth state to join the United States.

▶ America is divided into states. What other divisions are countries divided into?

▶ Why are countries divided into different parts? Do you think this is a good idea? Why or why not?

▶ Find out when the area you live in became a part of your country.

Long before CDs, music was recorded and played on records. Vinyl records were introduced in 1949.

▶ How many definitions of the word record can you identify?

Is the pronunciation always the same?

▶ Compact discs and records are round. How many other round things can you name?

▶ How else can music be recorded?

Today is International Thank-You Day.

▸ Name several ways that you can express thanks.

▸ Has someone done something nice for you recently? What is the nicest compliment you've ever received? What is the kindest thing you have ever done for someone?

▸ How do you say "thank you" in other languages?

Charles Perrault was born in Paris, France. Mr. Perrault worked as a lawyer, a supervisor of royal buildings, and a poet. Then he began to write fairy tales. His *Tales from Olden Times*, published in 1697, included "Cinderella" and "Little Red Riding Hood."

▸ Explain the difference between a tail and a tale.

▸ What is your favorite fairy tale? Why?

▸ Famous fairy tales may have several versions. Choose a fairy tale and see how many different versions you can find.

In 1957 the Wham-O Company produced the first Frisbee. Developed by Walter Frederick Morrison, the plastic disk was first called the Wham-O Pluto Platter. Over one hundred million Frisbees have been sold all over the world.

▶ What words can you use to describe how a Frisbee moves through the air?

▶ "Frisbee" is a name made up to describe a plastic flying saucer. It is now listed in the dictionary. Think of a new name for something you use. Tell why you think the new name is a good one.

▶ Find information about the World Flying Disc Federation.

Albert Schweitzer was born on July 14, 1875, in Germany. Until he was thirty, he studied theology and music. Then he became a medical missionary. He established a clinic in Gabon, Africa, and spent the next fifty years fighting leprosy and sleeping sickness.

▶ What is a missionary? Dr. Schweitzer is known as a humanitarian. What is a humanitarian?

▶ How can you help other people?

▶ What famous award did Dr. Schweitzer receive? Why?

Dr. Martin Luther King, Jr., was born in 1929. He was a good student and finished high school two years early. He went to college when he was 15. As a leader in the field of human rights, Dr. King believed in nonviolence.

▶ What do equality and nonviolence mean?

▶ Rev. King had a dream that all people would be treated equally regardless of their skin color. Do you think that his dream has been realized? Why or why not? What is your dream for the world?

▶ In 1963 Dr. King led a march on Washington, D.C. What was the purpose of this march? What do people remember about it?

Dian Fossey was born in 1932. An American zoologist, Dian undertook a long-term field study of wild gorillas in Rwanda. Her book, *Gorillas in the Mist*, describes her experiences.

▶ Due mainly to Fossey's research and conservation work, mountain gorillas are protected today. What does protected mean? What is conservation?

▶ Do you think it's a good idea to protect endangered animals? Why or why not?

▶ Find out more about Dian Fossey's life in Rwanda.

In 1706 Benjamin Franklin was born in Boston. Ben Franklin is important to American history as a scientist, statesman, printer, musician, an inventor, and an economist.

▶ Franklin was the editor and publisher of *Poor Richard's Almanac*. What is an almanac?

▶ Many sayings have been attributed to Franklin's almanac. Explain the meaning of these famous sayings:

Eat to live, don't live to eat.

A penny saved is a penny earned.

Early to bed and early to rise makes a man healthy, wealthy, and wise.

One today is worth two tomorrows.

▶ Find out about some of the things Benjamin Franklin invented.

Happy Birthday, A. A. Milne! Milne was born in London in 1882. He wrote verses and stories for his son, Christopher Robin. The characters, including Winnie the Pooh, Piglet, and Eeyore, are loved by children and adults.

▶ What words would you use to describe Winnie the Pooh? Piglet? Tiger?

▶ Which A. A. Milne character is your favorite? Why?

▶ What parts of A. A. Milne's stories are real? Imaginary?

In 1825 Ezra Daggett and Thomas Kensett were awarded a patent for storing food in tin cans.

▶ What is a patent?

▶ Why is storing food in tin cans helpful?

▶ What are food storage cans made of today?

The first radio broadcast of *The Lone Ranger* aired on Detroit's WXYZ in 1933. A Texas Ranger who was the sole survivor of an ambush by outlaws, the Lone Ranger vowed to bring justice to the West. The radio series continued weekly broadcasts until 1954.

▶ What is an ambush? A broadcast?

▶ *The Lone Ranger* television series aired from 1949 until 1957. How would a television series differ from a radio series?

▶ Find out what famous music was the Lone Ranger's theme song.

On January 21, 1799, Edward Jenner introduced a vaccination to prevent smallpox. He gave his patients fluid from a cowpox blister to help them build up an immunity against human smallpox. He named this procedure "vaccination" after the Latin word **vacca**, meaning "cow."

▶ What does **vaccinate** mean? What does **immunity** mean?

▶ What types of vaccinations do children routinely receive today?

▶ Is smallpox still a problem today? Why or why not?

Wilma Rudolph set a world's record for the women's indoor 60-yard dash. Her time was 6.9 seconds.

▶ What does **dash** mean? Tell about a time when you have made a dash.

▶ Most track-and-field events are held outdoors. Why would a meet be held indoors? What would be different about an indoor meet?

▶ Learn more about Wilma Rudolph. What other records did she hold? What obstacles did she overcome to become a champion?

Today is National Handwriting Day in the U.S. in honor of John Hancock's birthday in 1737. His signature was the largest signature on the Declaration of Independence.

▶ What is a signature? Give several different meanings of the word sign.

▶ This day is intended to encourage neat handwriting. What things can you do to make sure your handwriting is neat?

▶ How many people signed the Declaration of Independence?

On January 24, 1848, James Marshall discovered gold at John Sutter's mill in northern California. Gold fever swept the country.

By the end of the year, there were more than 10,000 prospectors in the fields.

▶ What is a prospector? What kind of a field has gold in it?

▶ Explain what you think is meant by gold fever. Have you ever had a "fever" like gold fever? What was it?

▶ Find out more about the role the discovery of gold played in the westward movement in U.S. history.

The first Winter Olympics took place in 1924 in Chamonix, France. At first the competition was not given Olympic status. It was simply called International Sports Week 1924. A total of 258 athletes from 16 nations participated in 16 events.

▶ What are Olympic games and events? Use the two words in sentences about the Olympics.

▶ Do you think participation in international sports competitions is a good idea? Why or why not?

▶ What sporting events are highlighted during the Winter Olympics? Which is your favorite? Why?

Maria Augusta Kutschera was born in Vienna, Austria. In 1926 she became the governess to the children of Baron Georg von Trapp and married Georg in 1927. Her story inspired the musical *The Sound of Music*.

▶ What is a governess? What synonyms can you think of for governess?

▶ In this instance, real people inspired a story. What other stories do you know that were inspired by real people?

▶ Learn more about Maria Augusta Kutschera and Georg von Trapp. Where did the von Trapp family live after they left Austria?

Wolfgang Amadeus Mozart was born in 1756 in Salzburg, Austria. He was a child prodigy, beginning to play instruments at age 4. His first performance was at age 6.

▶ What is a prodigy? What makes a prodigy special?

▶ Mozart is one of the greatest composers. What does a composer do?

▶ Listen to one of Mozart's compositions. Describe how it makes you feel.

In 1986 the space shuttle *Challenger* exploded 73 seconds after liftoff. All seven of its crew members were killed, including the first teacher in space, S. Christa McAuliffe.

▶ What does the word challenger mean? Do you think *Challenger* was a good name for a space shuttle?

▶ Do you think space exploration is important? Why or why not?

▶ What are the names of other space shuttles? What name would you give to a space shuttle? Why?

The first election to select players to be honored in the Baseball Hall of Fame was held in 1936. Members of the Baseball Writers' Association selected five charter Hall of Fame members: Ty Cobb, Babe Ruth, Honus Wagner, Christy Matheson, and Walter Johnson.

▶ What is fame?

▶ How would you explain the game of baseball to someone who had never played or seen this game before?

▶ Find a list of all the members in the Baseball Hall of Fame. Choose one and find out why that person was chosen for the honor.

In 1790 Henry Greathead tested his new invention, the lifeboat, at sea. His first prototype was named *The Original*.

▶ What is a lifeboat?

▶ Is it important to have a lifeboat on board a ship? Why or why not?

▶ What other safety precautions are available for travelers?

January 31

In 1928, 3M put transparent tape on the market. Richard G. Drew invented the tape to seal cellophane food wrap. The public found hundreds of uses for the new tape at work and at home.

- ▶ Drew's new tape was transparent, adhesive, and moisture-proof. Think of other adjectives that describe transparent tape.

- ▶ List the ways you use tape.

- ▶ John Borden designed the first tape dispenser with a built-in blade in 1932. What other improvements have been made to transparent tape since it was first introduced?

Black History Month

Library Lovers' Month

Children's Dental Health Month

Wild Bird Feeding Month

February

In 1709 Alexander Selkirk, a Scottish sailor, was rescued from the deserted island where he had lived alone for five years. His story became the basis for Daniel Defoe's book *Robinson Crusoe*.

▶ Define deserted island.

▶ What would you do to survive if you were stranded alone on a deserted island? What would you most miss about home? What five things would you want to have with you? Why?

▶ Choose an island. Find five facts about the island. Would you like to live there? Why or why not?

Happy Groundhog Day! Folklore has it that if the groundhog sees its shadow today, there will be six more weeks of winter; if it doesn't see its shadow, spring will arrive early.

▶ Define shadow. How is a shadow formed?

▶ Are you hoping that the groundhog does or does not see its shadow? Why?

▶ Find out more about groundhogs. What do they look like? What do they eat? Where do they live?

Today in Japan, Setsubun, the Bean-Throwing Festival celebrates the beginning of spring. Each person eats one bean for every year of life plus one for luck in the coming year. At public ceremonies, celebrities throw beans into the crowd. It's good luck to catch one.

▶ Give several synonyms for festival.

▶ What do you do for good luck? Does it really help?

▶ Find out more about other Japanese holidays.

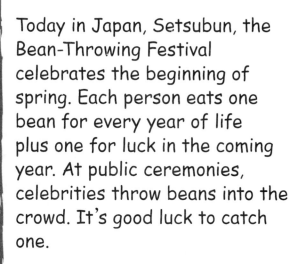

George Washington was unanimously elected the first U.S. president in 1789. All 690 presidential electors voted for him.

▶ Can you think of a synonym for **elect**? What does unanimously mean?

▶ What do you think makes a good leader? Did George Washington have any of these traits?

▶ The leader of the United States is the president. Name some other countries that have presidents. Name some other titles of country leaders.

In 1901 Ed Prescot patented the loop-the-loop roller coaster.

▸ What words would you use to describe a roller coaster ride?

▸ What makes a roller coaster exciting?

▸ Find the names of famous roller coasters. How do you think the names were chosen?

In 1935 the board game Monopoly™ went on sale for the first time. Charles B. Darrow of Germantown, Pennsylvania, developed the game. Parker Brothers didn't want the game, so Mr. Darrow began making and selling the game on his own.

▸ What does the word **monopoly** mean? Is Monopoly a good name for a game about buying and selling property? Tell why or why not.

▸ Make a list of board games. What is your favorite board game? Why?

▸ Find out more about the time around 1935, when Monopoly was introduced. What was life like for the average person? Did this have anything to do with the success of Monopoly?

John Deere, the inventor of the steel plow, was born in 1804.

▶ What do the words deer and dear mean? Can you use each word in a sentence? What are words that sound the same and have different spellings called?

▶ What was the importance of the steel plow?

▶ Name other agricultural inventions. How did they make farming easier?

Jules Verne was born February 8, 1839. At age 11, Jules ran off to sea. When he returned home he promised his family that he would adventure only in his imagination. He wrote 60 adventure novels including *Twenty Thousand Leagues Under the Sea.*

▶ What does the expression ran off to sea mean?

▶ Would you rather travel by land or by sea? Why?

▶ Jules Verne predicted some modern inventions in his books. Name some of them.

In 1864 U.S. President Abraham Lincoln posed for the photograph that is used for his image on the U.S. five-dollar bill.

- ▶ We use many different words for money. List as many words as you can.

- ▶ Images of other famous people are used on currency. Choose one of these people and tell why or why not he or she was a good choice.

- ▶ Find out about the money of a country other than your own. If someone's portrait is used on the money, tell who and why.

Famous cartoon pair Tom and Jerry debuted in 1940. This cat and mouse pair were created by William Hanna, an engineer, and Joseph Barbera, an accountant.

- ▶ What is a cartoon? How is an animated cartoon different from a real-life movie?

- ▶ What is your favorite cartoon? Why?

- ▶ Tom and Jerry in *Puss Gets the Boot* were nominated for an Academy Award in 1940. Find out some of the ways the pair has changed in the more than 60 years since their creation.

I smell a mouse about!

Today is National Inventors' Day. The day honors Thomas Alva Edison, born in 1847. He invented the electric light, the phonograph, the motion picture camera, and many other things.

▶ The suffix *-or* is added to the root word **invent** to form the word **inventor**— a person who invents. Give other words that add *-or*, *-ar*, *-ist*, and *-er* to name what a person does.

▶ What characteristics do you think all inventors have in common?

▶ Find out more about another famous inventor.

The sixteenth president of the United States, Abraham Lincoln, was born on this day in 1809. He was nicknamed Honest Abe.

▶ What does it mean to be honest? What does honesty mean to you?

▶ Can you describe a situation in which it would be difficult to be honest?

▶ What evidence can you find that proves Abe's honesty?

What Happened Today? • EMC 1015

Happy Birthday, Chuck Yeager! Mr. Yeager was the first aviator to fly faster than the speed of sound in 1947.

- ▶ What is an aviator?

- ▶ Sound travels very quickly. Name other things that travel fast.

- ▶ What is the speed of sound?

Happy Valentine's Day! This is a special holiday when we show people how much we like them.

- ▶ List nicknames that tell people you like them.

- ▶ Describe someone who is dear to you.

- ▶ How did the celebration of Valentine's Day begin?

In 1797 piano manufacturer Henry E. Steinway was born. His pianos continue to be known as excellent instruments.

▶ What is a stringed instrument? List several stringed instruments.

▶ What musical instrument would you like to play? Why?

▶ Describe several different types of pianos. Tell how they are similar and how they are different.

Today is Edgar Bergen's birthday. Mr. Bergen was a famous ventriloquist. He created his wooden dummy, Charlie McCarthy, when he was in high school.

▶ What is a ventriloquist? What does it mean to throw your voice?

▶ How is a ventriloquist different from a puppeteer?

▶ Find out about another famous ventriloquist.

Rene Laënnec, inventor of the stethoscope, was born in 1781.

▶ How would you describe a **stethoscope**? What does it look like? What is its purpose?

▶ Besides a stethoscope, can you name ten things associated with a doctor?

▶ Choose another medical tool. Find out who invented it and how it is used.

Alessandro Volta, inventor of the battery, was born in 1745.

▶ What is a **battery**?

▶ Can you name at least five things that run on batteries?

▶ How is a battery's power measured?

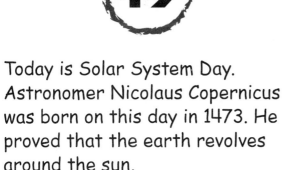

Today is Solar System Day. Astronomer Nicolaus Copernicus was born on this day in 1473. He proved that the earth revolves around the sun.

▶ What do the words astronomer, solar system, and universe mean?

▶ Can you name all the planets in our solar system? Which planet would you want to explore? Why?

▶ Find out more about Nicolaus Copernicus.

Automobile manufacturer Enzo Ferrari was born in 1898.

▶ What is a synonym for automobile?

▶ Besides a Ferrari, can you name ten other kinds of cars?

▶ Find out more about the history of the automobile.

In 1995 Steve Fossett became the first person to make a solo balloon flight across the Pacific. He started in South Korea and he landed in Leader, Saskatchewan.

- ▶ What does the word **solo** mean? Name some other kinds of solos.

- ▶ Would you like to ride in a hot-air balloon? Why or why not?

- ▶ How does the pilot of a hot-air balloon control the balloon?

Happy Birthday, George Washington, first president of the United States! He was born in Virginia in 1732.

- ▶ George Washington is the namesake of the capital of the United States. What is a **namesake**?

- ▶ Learning was important to George. He studied spelling, handwriting, geography, astronomy, arithmetic, and surveying. Do the subjects you study differ from his studies?

- ▶ In addition to being the first president of the United States, George Washington made important contributions to the development of the United States. Find out about some of these contributions.

The first bathtub was installed in the White House in 1851. Millard Fillmore was the president.

▶ Give several synonyms for the word clean.

▶ Take a survey of your classmates. Do they prefer the bathtub or the shower? Graph the results of your survey.

▶ Learn about the history of bathtubs. How have they changed over the years?

Wilhelm Carl Grimm was born on this day in 1786. He and his brother Jacob collected folktales and recorded them in several books. Today they are known as *Grimms' Fairy Tales*.

▶ Tale and tail are homonyms. Explain the difference in their meaning.

▶ Choose a character from your favorite fairy tale. What words would you use to describe this character?

▶ Make a list of tales included in *Grimms' Fairy Tales*.

         What Happened Today? • EMC 1015

The first performing monkey in America was exhibited in New York City. Admission to see the trained monkey was one cent.

- ▶ Explain what a trained animal is.

- ▶ Do you think animals should be trained to perform for audiences? Why or why not?

- ▶ Find out more about methods of training animals.

Dr. John Kellogg was born in 1852. He developed breakfast cereals and established the Battle Creek Toasted Corn Flake Company.

- ▶ Breakfast is a compound word. Tell the two words that are combined and give their meanings.

- ▶ Give step-by-step directions for preparing a bowl of cereal.

- ▶ List as many cereals as you can. Think of categories and group the cereals into the categories.

Happy Birthday, Chelsea Clinton! (1980) Chelsea is the daughter of former U.S. President Bill Clinton and Hillary Rodham Clinton.

► The wife of a president is called the First Lady. What name would you give the child of a president?

► What advantages and disadvantages would there be to being the president's child? Would you like it if your father or mother were president? Why or why not?

► What other former U.S. presidents have had children that grew up in the White House?

On February 28, 1849, passengers on board the first regularly scheduled steamboat from the East Coast of the U.S. to the West Coast via Cape Horn arrived in San Francisco. The steamboat left New York Harbor on October 6, 1848.

► The voyage lasted 4 months and 21 days. What words would you use to describe the length of the trip?

► Have you ever ridden on a steamboat? Would you like to spend four months on a steamboat? Why or why not?

► Trace the route of the steamboat on a map. Figure out about how many miles the steamboat traveled.

Happy Leap Year Day!

▶ What synonyms can you think of for the word leap?

▶ A leap year occurs once every four years. What happens if you're born on February 29?

▶ What famous people have leap-year birthdays?

It takes the earth 365.24219 days to make one cycle around the sun. To keep the calendar in line with the length of the earth's orbit around the sun, every four years one day is added to February. This 366-day year is called a leap year.

Actually, if the year is the last year of a century—1700, 1800, 1900, 2000—then it is only a leap year if it is exactly divisible by 400. 1900 was not a leap year, but 2000 was.

March

Music in
Our Schools Month

National
Umbrella
Month

National Women's
History Month

National Nutrition
Month

On March 1, 1872, Yellowstone National Park became the first national park in the world. There are more geysers and hot springs in the park than anywhere else in the world.

▶ What is a geyser? A hot spring?

▶ Have you ever visited a national park? Are all national parks the same? What do visitors to national parks do?

▶ Locate Yellowstone National Park on a map. Learn about some of its attractions.

Today is Cat in the Hat Day. Theodor S. Geisel, better known as Dr. Seuss, was born on this day in 1904. *The Cat in the Hat* is one of his famous rhyming books.

▶ Dr. Seuss is a pen name. What is a pen name?

▶ Choose any animal. Think of words that rhyme with the animal's name. Think of a rhyming story title for a story about your animal.

▶ Why did Theodor Geisel use the pseudonym Dr. Seuss? Did he use any other pseudonyms? What other authors use pen names?

In Japan, today is Hina Matsuri, the doll festival. The third of every March, Japanese homes display special dolls that have been passed from generation to generation. Friends and families visit each other to admire the dolls.

▶ What does the expression handed down mean?

▶ What family treasures has your family handed down?

▶ There are many kinds of dolls. Find out about several different kinds from several different countries.

Composer Antonio Vivaldi was born in 1678. His best-known work is *The Four Seasons*.

▶ Complete this syllogism:

composer : music ::
_____ : literature

▶ Listen to a recording of *The Four Seasons*. Describe the music and the way it makes you feel.

▶ What is your favorite song? Who is your favorite composer?

Annie Oakley broke all existing records for women's trap shooting. She smashed 98 of 100 clay targets.

▶ What is a target? In addition to trap shooting, when might you use a target?

▶ Have you ever tried to hit a target? What did you use to hit it? Was it easy or difficult? What did you do so that you would be successful?

▶ Annie Oakley was part of Buffalo Bill Cody's Wild West Show. Discover some interesting facts about Annie Oakley or Buffalo Bill.

In 1930 Clarence Birdseye sold the first frozen foods.

▶ What does frozen mean? Think of words you would use to describe something that is frozen.

▶ Name ten things you would find in the frozen food section of a grocery store.

▶ What other ways is food preserved? Compare these methods with freezing. Which do you think is better? Why?

 What Happened Today? • EMC 1015

In 1985 the song *We Are the World* was played on the radio for the first time. Forty-five of pop music's top stars combined their talents to record the music of Lionel Richie and Michael Jackson. The proceeds from the multimillion-selling recording went to aid African famine victims.

▶ What is a famine?

▶ Do you think that it is important to use your talents to help other people? Why or why not?

▶ Read the words of *We Are the World.* Choose one line and use it to make a banner.

In 1855 the *London,* a 23-ton locomotive, was the first to cross the Niagara Gorge Bridge. John Roebling designed the railway suspension bridge. It spanned Niagara Falls, connecting Canada and the U.S.

▶ What does suspension mean?

▶ What are the different ways you could cross Niagara Falls? Which way do you think is best? Why?

▶ What other structures did John Roebling design?

Ruth Handler watched her daughter Barbara play and then developed the idea for a teen fashion doll. She named the doll after her daughter, and Barbie made her debut at the Toy Fair in New York City in 1959.

▶ Many people collect Barbie dolls. What is a collection?

▶ There are many different Barbie dolls, such as gymnastic Barbie dolls, beach Barbie dolls, and bridal Barbie dolls. What kind of Barbie doll would you create? Describe the special clothes and accessories you would include with the doll.

▶ Choose another toy. Find out when it was created and by whom.

The United States issued paper money for the first time in 1862.

▶ What is money?

▶ What are the advantages and disadvantages of paper money?

▶ Find out what early forms of money were used. Describe the changes in money that have occurred over time.

American pioneer John Chapman, better known as Johnny Appleseed, died in 1845. He was famous for planting apple trees throughout the Midwest.

- ▶ What is a pioneer?

- ▶ What can you do with an apple?

- ▶ Find out more about John Chapman's life. What parts of Johnny Appleseed's story are true?

In 1894 Coca-Cola™ was sold in bottles for the first time.

- ▶ Coca-Cola™ can be called soda or pop. What else does the word pop mean? Write a sentence for each of the different meanings you know.

- ▶ A bottle is a type of container. In addition to Coca-Cola,™ what else comes in a bottle?

- ▶ How was Coca-Cola,™ sold before it came in bottles? What advantages and disadvantages did the bottles have?

In 1781 Astronomer William Herschel discovered the planet Uranus. On this day in 1930, Astronomer Clyde Tombaugh discovered the planet Pluto.

▶ What is a planet?

▶ Would you like to travel in space? Why or why not?

▶ Choose a planet. Read about it. List five facts.

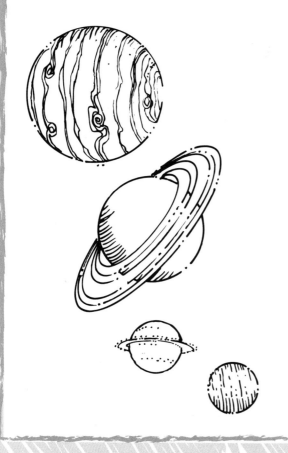

In 1794 Eli Whitney received his patent for the cotton gin. His invention, made it possible to clean 50 pounds of cotton per day. Before the invention, only one pound of cotton was cleaned per day.

▶ Eli Whitney's cotton gin increased productivity. What does that mean?

▶ What is the result of increased productivity? Can you think of a time that you have increased your own productivity? Explain.

▶ Eli Whitney's invention is part of the Industrial Revolution, when machines started to do work that had been done by hand. Think of a place where machines do a job that could be done by hand. Explain how using the machine has increased productivity.

Finns and Lapps come together to see the Reindeer Driving Competition at Inari. Men and women compete in the sport of driving reindeer herds.

▶ What is a herd? What kinds of herds have you seen? What does it mean to drive a herd?

▶ Some animals are wild and some are domestic. What is the difference? Why are some animals domesticated?

▶ What is the reindeer's natural habitat?

Dr. Robert Goddard, an American scientist, fired the first liquid-fuel rocket in 1926. The rocket was less than 12 feet tall, but it launched the space age.

▶ What is the space age? What words are associated with space travel?

▶ Is it important to travel in space? Why or why not?

▶ Find out more about Dr. Goddard. Compile your information into a short biography.

Happy St. Patrick's Day! This celebration is noted for parades, "wearin' o' the green," and good fellowship. Legend has it that if you catch one of the little people, called leprechauns, who join in the celebration, he must grant you three wishes.

▶ What is a legend?

▶ If you caught a leprechaun, what three things would you wish for? What would you do if you found a pot of gold at the end of a rainbow?

▶ Find out about St. Patrick. Who was he? Why do the Irish have a feast in his honor?

The Ibo people of Nigeria celebrate the end of their year. At a specific moment everyone makes noise to symbolize grief over the end of the old year. Children run into their homes and bang the doors as loudly as they can. When the sounds fade away, everyone rushes outside and welcomes the New Year with applause.

▶ What is applause? Can you applaud something without making any noise? Explain.

▶ List all the times you have heard applause.

▶ Read more about Nigeria and the Ibo people.

The swallows return to San Juan Capistrano in California. Every year hundreds of swallows return to their nests in and near the famous Mission San Juan Capistrano. They remain there until about October 23.

▶ Give several synonyms for return.

▶ Legend suggests that the swallows sought sanctuary at the mission when an innkeeper destroyed their nests. They return to nest each year knowing that their nests will be safe. Do you think the legend is true? Why or why not?

▶ Are there other animals that follow specific, yearly routines? Read about the buzzards in Hinckley, Ohio. Can you find others?

It's Mitsumasa Anno's birthday! Mitsumasa Anno was born in 1926 in Tsuwano, a remote town in Japan. As a child he wondered what life was like in other parts of the world. As an adult he creates many different worlds in his children's books.

▶ Mitsumasa Anno is an author and an illustrator, a mathematician, and an artist. Explain what each of those words means.

▶ If you were going to create a visual record of the world of your classroom, what images would you include? Why?

▶ Find and read one of Anno's books.

Kate Smith recorded the song "God Bless America." Immigrant Irving Berlin wrote the song in 1918 as a tribute to his adopted country, the United States.

▶ What is an immigrant?

▶ Mr. Berlin donated all of his royalties from "God Bless America" to the Boy Scouts. What are royalties? Why do you think he did that? Have you ever made a donation?

▶ Read the words of "God Bless America." Tell how Mr. Berlin felt about his adopted country.

Happy Birthday, Marcel Marceau! Born in France, Mr. Marceau loved to pantomime. As an adult he entertained audiences as a mime.

▶ What is pantomime? What does a mime do?

▶ Think of something you could pantomime. Try it out!

▶ Find out how most mimes dress. Why do you think they dress as they do?

23

In 1857 the E. G. Otis Company completed installation of the world's first commercial passenger elevator in a store in New York City.

▶ What is the root word of elevator? Think of other words that come from the same root word.

▶ Have you ever ridden in an elevator? How would you describe an elevator to someone who had never seen one? What would you do if you were stuck on an elevator?

▶ Find out more about the invention and use of elevators.

24

At four minutes past midnight in 1989, the supertanker *Exxon Valdez* ran aground in Prince William Sound, Alaska. Over 11.2 million gallons of oil were spilled.

▶ What does aground mean? What is a supertanker? What other "super" words can you think of? What do they mean?

▶ Why are oil spills a problem?

▶ Find out more about the consequences of the *Exxon Valdez* oil spill.

Sculptor Gutzon Borglum was born in 1871. He is best known for carving the national memorial Mount Rushmore. He sculpted the busts of Presidents George Washington, Thomas Jefferson, Theodore Roosevelt, and Abraham Lincoln in the granite slopes of the Black Hills of South Dakota.

▶ What is a sculptor?

▶ A new sculptor is deciding on heads to be carved in a new monument. Whose heads do you think should be included? Why?

▶ Find other sculptures in your area. Who did the sculptures? What do the sculptures represent or honor?

Happy Birthday, Robert Frost! This famous American poet was born in San Francisco in 1874. When he was 11, he moved to Massachusetts. He worked as a journalist, a farmer, and a teacher before devoting himself to his poetry.

▶ Tell what the words poem, poet, and poetic mean. What is the difference between a poem and a story?

▶ Robert Frost wrote,

"Two roads diverged in a wood, and I took the one less traveled by, And that has made all the difference."

Which road would you take? Explain why.

▶ Find and read a poem written by Robert Frost.

Kindergarten teacher Patty Smith Hill was born in 1868. She is credited with composing the song "Happy Birthday To You."

▸ **Birthday** is a compound word. What other compound word describes a holiday?

▸ Name 10 things associated with a birthday.

▸ How are birthdays celebrated in different parts of the world?

In Czechoslovakia children celebrate the birthday of Jan Amos Komensky by taking flowers to their teachers. In 1658 Mr. Komensky was the first person to write a book for children only. The book included woodcut illustrations because Mr. Komensky believed that children could learn words by looking at pictures.

▸ What is an **illustration**? An **illustrator**?

▸ Do you think picture books are important? Why or why not?

▸ Use the card catalog or database to locate your favorite picture book. Record the title, illustrator, and year it was published.

Happy birthday to you!

Denton True Young was born on March 29, 1867. His nickname changed from *Dent* to *Cy* (for *cyclone*) when he became a major league pitcher. Cy Young pitched 511 wins in 22 seasons, the most by any pitcher ever. Today's annual award for the best pitcher is named for him.

▶ What is a pitcher?

▶ Cy got his nickname because of his blinding fastball—it was like a cyclone. Do any of your friends have nicknames? How did they get them?

▶ Find out more about Cy Young's amazing career as a major league pitcher.

In 1858 Hyman Lipman invented the first pencil with an eraser.

▶ Name all the parts of a pencil.

▶ What would you like to erase? Why? How would you do it?

▶ Find out about the invention of another tool you use in school.

It is said that the month of March comes in like a lion and goes out like a lamb.

▶ What worlds would you use to descibe a lion? a lamb?

▶ What do you think the expression "in like a lion and out like a lamb" means? How does it relate to spring weather?

▶ Find out about another weather expression and how it came to be.

April

Keep America Beautiful Month

Mathematics Education Month

National Poetry Month

ZAM! Zoo and Aquarium Month

Today is April Fools' Day, or All Fools' Day. It is a tradition to pull a prank on someone or joke with someone today and then say, "April Fool!"

▶ What is a prank? What does it mean to be foolish or do something foolish?

▶ Watch out! People may "pull your leg" today. What does that expression mean? What could you do if someone "pulls your leg"?

▶ French fisherman say that early spring is a time when young fish are easier to catch than older fish, so an easily tricked person is called an April fish—*poisson d'avril*. French children are given chocolate fish candies on April 1. Find out about another holiday tradition that has a connection to an event in nature.

Today is International Children's Book Day and the birthday of Hans Christian Andersen (1805). He wrote children's fairy tales, including "The Ugly Duckling."

▶ A duckling is a baby duck. Do you know what the babies of cats, dogs, rabbits, bears, deer, cows, kangaroos, goats, sheep, and frogs are called?

▶ If you could be a character from a fairy tale, which character would you want to be? Why?

▶ Create a list of the stories Hans Christian Andersen wrote. Learn more about his life.

Washington Irving, author of *Rip Van Winkle*, was born in 1783. In the story, Rip Van Winkle falls asleep and sleeps for 20 years. When he awakens, great changes have taken place in the world.

► List verbs that could be used in talking about sleeping and waking.

► If you fell asleep for the next 20 years (beginning today), what changes do you think you'd find when you woke up?

► Find out what was happening 20 years ago today.

In 1818 the Congress of the United States limited the number of stripes on the American flag to thirteen and declared that a star be added for each new state.

► The words flag and star can be used as actions and to name things. Think of two sentences using the words in different ways.

► How many of the stripes are red on the American flag? White? What do the thirteen stripes represent? How many stars are there?

► Choose the flag of a country, state, or province. Tell what the symbols on the flag mean.

5

Booker T. Washington, an African-American son of slaves, was born on April 5, 1856, in Virginia. He became a teacher and the director of one of the leading African-American educational institutions, Tuskegee Normal and Industrial Institute in Alabama.

► Booker T. Washington was a pioneer in education. What is a pioneer? What does it mean to be a pioneer in education?

► Booker T. Washington was an eloquent speaker. What characteristics are important to good speaking?

► Create a time line of important events in Booker T. Washington's life. Which event do you think is the most important? Why?

6

In 1909 explorers Admiral Robert Peary and Matthew Hensen became the first people to reach the North Pole. Admiral Peary led many expeditions to the Pole and Greenland.

► What do the words explore and expedition mean?

► Admiral Peary had to follow directions to get to the North Pole. Give directions for going from your house to the school and from your classroom to the lunchroom.

► What kinds of things did these explorers take on their expedition to the North Pole? Why?

The World Health Organization, an agency of the United Nations, has declared that today is World Health Day. The goal of the organization is to build a world of healthier people.

▶ What does it mean to be healthy?

▶ What things should you do to stay healthy?

▶ Choose one health problem. Find out what is being done to solve it.

Hana Matsuri, the flower festival, is celebrated today. There are parades and singing to celebrate the birthday of Buddha. Japanese legends say that when Buddha was born, flower petals fell from the sky. Those celebrating carry fresh flowers to Buddhist shrines.

▶ The petal is just one part of a flower. Name all the parts of a flower.

▶ What is your favorite flower? Why is it your favorite?

▶ Find out more about the Buddhist religion.

In 1770 Captain James Cook discovered Botany Bay. Before this no Europeans had visited the eastern coast of the recently discovered island of Australia. He first called the bay Stingray Bay, but he renamed it after a group of scientists found many unknown plant specimens growing on the shore.

▶ What is a specimen?

▶ Captain Cook is remembered as a world explorer. He is credited with helping mapmakers make accurate maps of the world. Why do you think Cook's explorations helped mapmakers make accurate maps?

▶ Find out more about Captain Cook's explorations.

Today in 1866 the American Society for Prevention of Cruelty to Animals was chartered. The ASPCA, founded by Henry Bergh, is still active today.

▶ What does prevention mean?

▶ What can you do to prevent cruelty to animals?

▶ Is there an ASPCA in your community? Is there a similar organization? Find out what the organizations are doing.

12

In 1928 the cartoon character Popeye appeared for the first time in a newspaper. Popeye was created by Elzie Crisler Segar.

- ► What is a cartoon? a comic strip? Explain the differences.

- ► If you could be in a comic strip or a cartoon, which one would it be? Why?

- ► Find out more about Popeye. How did he look? What kind of a guy was he? Do you think he was a positive role model?

At 10 a.m. on April 12, 1955, the announcement was made that a safe, effective vaccine had been found in the fight against polio, a crippling disease. The vaccine had been developed by Dr. Jonas Salk.

- ► What is a vaccine?

- ► Dr. Salk's polio vaccine is called a "milestone in medical history." What do you think that expression means? Why?

- ► Find out what vaccinations are commonly given to children and to adults.

Thomas Jefferson was born in 1743. He was the third president of the United States and the main author of the Declaration of Independence.

▶ What does it mean to be independent or to do things independently? What is the opposite of independent?

▶ In what ways are you independent?

▶ Find out more about the life of Thomas Jefferson. Do you think he demonstrated independence? Explain why or why not.

In 1828 Noah Webster published his *Dictionary of the English Language*.

▶ Write your own definition for the word dictionary.

▶ Why was Noah Webster's dictionary important? Why do you think the words in a dictionary are in alphabetical order? What other places can you find things in alphabetical order?

▶ Name all the different parts of a dictionary entry.

In 1955 Ray Kroc opened the first McDonald's in Des Plaines, Illinois. After visiting a California hamburger restaurant owned by the McDonald brothers, Mr. Kroc decided to open several restaurants serving this fast food.

▶ What is fast food?

▶ How many things can you name that are associated with McDonald's?

▶ What is McDonald's slogan? List other products and their slogans.

Aviator Wilbur Wright was born in 1867. He and his brother Orville invented the first powered aircraft. They flew it for 12 seconds on December 17, 1903, in Kitty Hawk, North Carolina.

▶ What other words can you use to name aircraft?

▶ What would life be like if people could fly? Would this be a good thing? Why or why not?

▶ Find out more about the Wrights' first flight in Kitty Hawk.

In 1492 Christopher Columbus signed a contract with a representative of King Ferdinand and Queen Isabella of Spain. Columbus was to find a westward ocean passage to Asia. The King and Queen would pay for the exploration.

▶ What is a contract?

▶ Do you think Columbus lived up to his part of the contract? Tell why or why not.

▶ Write a contract stating something you will do for someone and what you will get in return.

In 1775 Paul Revere made his famous ride from Boston to Lexington to warn people that the British soldiers were on their way. The next day the Battle of Lexington and Concord marked the beginning of the U.S. war for independence.

▶ List some synonyms for the word warn.

▶ Today in Boston, Paul Revere's ride is remembered with the running of the Boston Marathon. Do you think a marathon is a good way to remember this event? Why or why not?

▶ Paul Revere's ride is the subject of a famous poem by Longfellow. Read the poem. Identify the parts of the poem that are facts.

In 1982 the National Aeronautics and Space Administration (NASA) announced that Sally Ride had been selected as the first American woman astronaut.

▶ What is an astronaut? What are the meanings of the prefix astro- and the suffix –naut? What other "nauts" can you think of?

▶ If you could travel anywhere in space, where would you want to go? Why?

▶ Find out more about Sally Ride's life.

In 1865 safety matches were advertised for the first time. The matches were sold in small wooden boxes that had a chemical mixture painted on one edge. When the chemical tip of each small wooden splint was rubbed along the painted edge, the wood ignited.

▶ What does it mean to advertise something?

▶ How do advertisers decide what they will say about their products? Are all advertisements good? Explain why or why not.

▶ Choose a product. Write an advertisement for it.

Gideon Sundback patented the hookless fastener in 1913. The fastener was very much like today's zipper. It didn't get its name until 1923 when it was used in a style of rubber boots and the advertisers coined the name zipper. "Zip 'er up or zip 'er down."

▶ The word zip is an example of onomatopoeia, words that imitate the sounds of the things they name. How many other examples of onomatopoeia can you name?

▶ Give something in your classroom a name based on the sound associated with it. See if your classmates can guess what the thing is.

▶ What other fasteners were used before zippers? What new fasteners were invented after zippers?

In 1872 J. Sterling Morton believed a day should be set aside to plant trees and recognize their importance. He chose his birthday, April 22, for the original Arbor Day. Today Arbor Day is celebrated on different days in different places.

▶ Why is Arbor Day a good name for a holiday about trees?

▶ If there were no trees, what would the world be like?

▶ The first Earth Day, a day to focus on taking care of the earth and its resources, was held on April 22, 1970. List concerns that Arbor Day and Earth Day have in common.

In 1772 Claude Joseph Rouget de Lisle wrote France's national anthem. "La Marseillaise" is still proudly sung by the French citizens today.

▶ What is an anthem?

▶ How do you feel when you sing an anthem? What makes you feel that way?

▶ Listen to the "La Marseillaise." Does the music reflect special feelings?

In 1833 Jacob Ebert and George Dulty were awarded a patent for the soda fountain.

▶ What is a fountain? A soda fountain?

▶ Name as many different flavors of ice cream as you can.

▶ Find a recipe for an ice-cream soda. Try it out!

In 1990 the Hubble Space Telescope was placed into orbit by the shuttle *Discovery*.

▶ What is an orbit? Name some things that are in orbit.

▶ Do you think it is important to have a space station? Why or why not?

▶ Find out what requirements need to be met before a permanent manned space station is established.

Happy Birthday, John James Audubon! Mr. Audubon, born in 1785, was famous for his book *Birds of America*. He drew and painted birds in such detail that people used his drawings for identifying birds.

▶ Explain what these "bird" phrases mean.

  bird watcher

  strictly for the birds

  bird's-eye view

▶ Name as many different types of birds as you can.

▶ Find out about the National Audubon Society, the conservation organization named for John James Audubon.

Happy Birthday!

Samuel Morse, inventor of the International Morse Code and the telegraph, was born in 1791. Morse's code used a system of dots and dashes to send messages over the telegraph. It is still used today.

- ▸ What is a code? Have you ever used a code? Tell when.

- ▸ Think of ways to represent the dots and dashes in Morse's code. (He used electric impulses carried over a cable.) Encode a message and send it.

- ▸ Learn about other codes. Who created them? What were they used for? Are they still used today?

In 1947 Norwegian explorer Thor Heyerdahl set sail to cross the Pacific on a raft. He left the coast of Peru with a six-man crew on the 45-foot balsa wood Kon-Tiki. The voyage ended successfully 101 days later. The raft had traveled over 4,300 miles.

- ▸ The word coast has several different meanings. What does it mean in the phrase the coast of Peru? What other meanings do you know for the word?

- ▸ One way to move across water is to sail. Name as many other ways as you can. Which way would you like to travel? Why?

- ▸ Thor Heyerdahl wrote a famous book about his voyage. Find the book and read about some of his adventures.

In 1813 rubber was patented by J. F. Hummel of Philadelphia.

▸ Rubber can be used as an adjective. Name 10 things that it could describe.

▸ What are the advantages of a rubber boot compared to a leather boot? Which do you think is better? Why?

▸ Mr. Hummel was only one of the people who had rubber-related patents. Find out more about the history of rubber.

In 1952 the first toy was advertised on television. What toy was it? Mr. Potato Head! The original Mr. Potato Head consisted of little pieces that were put into a real potato.

▸ What is advertising?

▸ How would you describe Mr. Potato Head to someone who had never seen one?

▸ Choose a toy. When was it first introduced to the public? Write an advertisement for the toy.

National
Bike Month

National
Pet Week

National
Egg Month

Get Caught
Reading Month

May

1

May Day is one of the world's oldest holidays. It probably originated from a Roman celebration of spring. In modern celebrations May baskets are filled with flowers and hung on friends' doors.

▶ People gather flowers and tree branches and "bring in the May." What do you think the phrase "bring in the May" means?

▶ In old England people believed that you could make freckles disappear if you faced east and washed your face with dew before dawn on the first of May. What other beliefs or customs do you know?

▶ May Day is celebrated in different ways around the world. Choose a country and find out about its May Day celebration.

2

The first drawing to be faxed successfully across the Atlantic Ocean was transmitted on May 2, 1926. The fax, a sketch of Ambassador Alanson Bigelow Houghton, was sent from London to *The New York Times* offices in New York. The transmission took about an hour.

▶ What is a fax?

▶ A fax is one way that people can communicate. Compare a faxed message with a message sent by mail or by phone. What are the advantages and disadvantages of each?

▶ Learn more about new ways that people send messages to each other. Choose one and report on its advantages and disadvantages.

Margaret Thatcher became the first female Prime Minister in British history in 1979. Thatcher's three consecutive terms in office marked the longest term of a British Prime Minister in 150 years.

▶ What does the word consecutive mean? Name two things that are consecutive.

▶ Has your city, country, state, or province ever had a female leader? Why do you think many more leaders are male?

▶ Choose a famous woman leader and find out more about her.

In 1973 Bob Matern set the world record for eating hamburgers. He ate 83 in just $2\frac{1}{2}$ hours.

▶ A hamburger is a kind of sandwich. How many other sandwiches can you name?

▶ What kind of world record would you like to set?

▶ Look in a book of records. Find one record that is interesting to you and create a sign that gives information about the record and names the record holder.

5

Today is Kodomo-No-Hi, a day when Japanese families honor their children. It is sometimes called the Feast of Flags. One flag is flown for each child in the family. The flags, made in the shape of carp, fly from the roof or a tall pole set up in the garden.

▶ Think of synonyms for the verb honor.

▶ Carp are strong fish that swim up fast-moving streams. They symbolize courage. What animals do you know that symbolize human characteristics?

▶ Learn more about other Japanese holidays.

6

The world's first postage stamp was issued on May 6, 1840, in Great Britain. It was called "Penny Black" because it was printed in black and it cost a penny.

▶ The word stamp has many meanings. Give several and use each in a sentence.

▶ People collect many different things. What different things do you collect?

▶ Collectors often have special names. A stamp collector is called a philatelist. What do you call a coin collector? Find the names of other collectors.

Happy Birthday, Johannes Brahms! Brahms, born in 1833, was a composer. His most famous work is "Brahm's Lullaby."

▶ What is a lullaby?

▶ What is your favorite lullaby? What musical characteristics should a lullaby have? Justify your ideas.

▶ Learn more about Brahms' life. Listen to his famous lullaby.

Lullaby, tra, la!

Hernando de Soto was a Spanish explorer who led conquests of Central America and Peru. On May 8, 1564, as he led his soldiers through what would become the southeastern United States, they became the first Europeans to see the Mississippi River.

▶ In addition to a river, how many other bodies of water can you name?

▶ Do you think there are still discoveries to be made? Tell about a time that you explored a new place or made a discovery.

▶ Learn more about de Soto and his explorations.

9

On May 9, 1860, Sir James M. Barrie was born in Scotland. He was a famous author and playwright. His most famous play tells the story of a boy who would not grow up and who lived in a land of pirates and Indians—Peter Pan.

▶ What is the difference between an author and a playwright?

▶ Peter Pan lived in a land called Never-Never-Land. What would you name an imaginary land you lived in? What would it be like?

▶ Read a version of *Peter Pan*.

10

Hotel Statler in Boston, Massachusetts, installed radio headsets in 1,300 rooms. Starting on May 10, 1927, a central control room in the hotel broadcast two stations directly to the rooms.

▶ What is a headset? Have you ever used one? What other names do headsets have today?

▶ Have you ever stayed in a hotel? Did the hotel have radios? Televisions? In-room movies? Video games? Other in-room entertainment systems?

▶ Learn more about the development of the radio. Create a time line showing important dates.

Martha Graham was born in 1894. She was an innovative dancer and choreographer. She founded the Martha Graham School of Contemporary Dance in 1927. She danced throughout her life, performing her last dance on stage when she was 76.

▶ What is contemporary?

▶ What types of dance would you consider contemporary? Which is your favorite?

▶ Choose a favorite dancer and learn more about him or her.

Happy Birthday, Florence Nightingale! Born in 1820, Ms. Nightingale revolutionized nursing. She established a military hospital in Turkey to care for British soldiers. She believed that hospitals needed to be kept clean. Her changes saved the lives of many soldiers.

▶ What does a nurse do? What other people do similar things?

▶ Have you ever had to nurse anyone? Describe your experiences.

▶ Talk to someone who is a nurse. Find out about the current changes in nursing care.

13

Recording artist Stevie Wonder was born May 13, 1950. Blinded at birth, he doesn't let that stop him. At 11, he could play the piano, drums, and harmonica. His first album, recorded when he was 12, topped the record charts. He has performed and written music for people all over the world.

▶ Special words define the parts of a song. Tell what the following "song words" mean:

lyrics   melody
refrain   harmony

▶ Listen to one of Stevie Wonder's songs. What is the song saying? What kind of a mood does the song have?

▶ Choose a style of music and learn more about it.

14

Gabriel Fahrenheit, inventor of the mercury thermometer, was born in Poland in 1686. He developed the temperature scale that is still used in the United States today.

▶ As the mercury in the thermometer rises, it gets warmer. Think of as many synonyms for warm as you can.

▶ Why is a thermometer important? How do you use a thermometer?

▶ What other temperature scale is commonly used today? Compare it to the Fahrenheit scale. Which scale do you use?

15

On May 15, 1918, the first regular airmail service began in the U.S. The very first flight was delayed because the plane's gas tank was empty, the pilot got lost, and the plane landed in a field outside of Washington, D.C. The mail was returned by railroad and sent out again the next day.

- ► What does regular mean? Make a list of regular deliveries made to your school or home.

- ► Think of conditions and problems that might represent obstacles to regular airmail delivery. Then think of ways to overcome those obstacles.

- ► The planes used in the first airmail service, *Jennies*, were modified to carry 120 pounds of mail. Find out more about these planes.

16

In 1866 the U.S. Treasury Department added another coin to American currency by authorizing the minting of the nickel. The nickel would be worth five cents.

- ► What is currency? What does it mean to mint something?

- ► Why would a new coin be made? Why does the government decide what coins will be made?

- ► Examine a nickel. Note all of the information on the face and the reverse side.

17

In 1792, 24 merchants formed the New York Stock Exchange (NYSE). They signed an agreement to trade with one another under a buttonwood tree on Wall Street. Today over 3,000 companies are listed with the exchange.

▶ **Stock** is a word with several different meanings. What meanings in addition to the New York Stock Exchange can you think of?

▶ Have you ever had to **exchange** something? Tell about your experience.

▶ Newspapers publish the results of trading on the NYSE daily. Choose one stock and see how many shares were traded today. What was the price of one share?

18

Today in 1980 Mt. St. Helens blew its top. At 8:32 a.m. an earthquake beneath the volcano caused a major eruption.

▶ A volcano **erupts**. What does that mean? What other things might erupt?

▶ The explosion and lava flow from an eruption kill wildlife. What problems might this cause?

▶ Choose another volcano. Learn about its latest eruption.

In 1906, 53 boys' clubs joined together to form the Federated Boys' Club. The organization's mission was to inspire young people and provide a safe place for them to grow and learn. The organization, now called The Boys and Girls Clubs of America, serves over 3.3 million young people.

▶ Club has several different meanings. Explain the difference between the Boys and Girls Clubs and the clubs used in the sport of golf. Are there other meanings for the word club?

▶ Do you belong to any clubs? Do you think clubs serve an important purpose? Explain why you think the way you do.

▶ Choose a club. Learn about how the club started.

May 20 is the anniversary of the first solo flight across the Atlantic Ocean. In 1927 Charles Lindbergh took off from Long Island in the state of New York. After flying though sleet and snow, he landed in Paris, France, 33 hours and 39 minutes later.

▶ What is an anniversary?

▶ Charles Lindbergh made a solo flight. What does that mean? Have you ever performed a solo? Tell about it.

▶ Learn more about Lindbergh's plane, *The Spirit of St. Louis*.

21

In 1819 bicycles were seen on the streets of New York for the first time. The first bicycles were wooden "horses" known as swift walkers. The rider pushed his or her feet backward against the ground to propel the vehicle forward.

▶ What is the root word of **bicycle**? Tell other words with the same root.

▶ Why do you think the first bicycles were called **swift walkers**? Do you think this was a good name? Why or why not?

▶ It took 70 years for the bicycle to change from the wooden horse to today's bicycle. Learn more about some of the early bikes.

22

In 1967 *Mr. Rogers' Neighborhood* debuted on national television. Within a year it was broadcast nationwide. Mr. Rogers has welcomed young viewers to over 870 different episodes.

▶ What is a **neighborhood**?

▶ Have you ever watched *Mr. Rogers' Neighborhood* on television? Did you like the program? Why or why not?

▶ Choose a character from *Mr. Rogers' Neighborhood*. List characteristics that describe that character.

In 1873 Canada's Northwest Mounted Police force was established to bring law and order to the Northwest Territories. The organization later became the Royal Canadian Mounted Police, or the Mounties.

▶ What does the phrase law and order mean? Give examples of law and order in your classroom or community.

▶ Do you think that law and order are important to progress? Why or why not?

▶ The Mounties wear distinctive uniforms. Learn about what special things are included in their uniforms.

In 1869 John Wesley Powell, a one-armed Civil War veteran and professor, embarked on the first expedition down the Colorado River through the Grand Canyon. He led nine men in four boats, beginning in Green River, Wyoming.

▶ What is an **expedition**? What does it mean **to embark**?

▶ Imagine that you were embarking on a expedition. What things would be important to take with you?

▶ Learn more about the Grand Canyon and how it was formed. What is it like today?

In 1986 about 7 million Americans formed a line across the country in the Hands Across America event. Their efforts raised money for the country's homeless and hungry.

▶ What does it mean to **give someone a hand** or **lend a hand**?

▶ What can you do to help people that are hungry and homeless?

▶ Identify organizations in your community that help the homeless and the hungry. Find out exactly what they are doing.

In 1977 George Willig, also known as the Human Fly, did the impossible. He scaled the World Trade Center in New York City. He attached himself to a pulley and walked straight up. It took him $3\frac{1}{2}$ hours to make the climb.

▶ What does it mean to **scale** a building? To **scale** a fish? To play a **scale**?

▶ When Willig reached the top of the building, the police were there to arrest him. Do you think what he did was wrong? Tell why you think as you do.

▶ Use a book of records to find another person who has completed an unusual feat. Tell what that person did.

27

In 1790 Jeremiah Carlton went to bed. He stayed in bed for the next 70 years while servants took care of his every need. Mr. Carlton has been declared the laziest man in history.

▶ Define the word lazy. What is an antonym for lazy?

▶ Would you want to live your life like this man? Why or why not?

▶ Many books have been written that involve a bed. Use a keyword search to find a "bed book." Read the book and report on it.

28

In 1959 two monkeys, Able and Baker, zoomed 300 miles into space on a Jupiter missile. They became the first animals retrieved from a space mission.

▶ What does it mean to be retrieved? Tell something you might retrieve.

▶ Why do you think that scientists sent monkeys into space?

▶ Find out if other animals have been space travelers.

In 1953 Edmund Hillary, a climber from New Zealand, and Tensing Norkdy, a Nepalese mountaineer, became the first climbers to reach the top of Mt. Everest, the tallest mountain in the world.

▶ How would you describe a **mountain** to someone who had never seen one?

▶ Would you want to be a mountain climber? Tell why or why not.

▶ Learn specific details about Hillary and Norkdy's ascent.

Today is Memorial Day in the United States. It is a day to remember men and women who fought and died in defense of the United States.

▶ What is a **memorial**? What is the root word of memorial?

▶ Why is it important that we remember and honor people? Is there someone that you honor? Tell why.

▶ The May 30 Memorial Day is a U.S. holiday. How do other countries honor their heroes?

31

Today is World No Tobacco Day. The day is sponsored by the World Health Organization's Tobacco Free Initiative. The initiative was established in 1998 because the World Health Organization (WHO) believes that the use of tobacco is an important public health issue.

▸ When something is called public, what does that mean? What is public health?

▸ Why do you think the WHO considers tobacco use a public health issue? Do you agree? Tell why.

▸ Throughout the world, tobacco use is predicted to cause one death in eight in the next decade. Learn more about the impact of tobacco on health. Make a poster that shows what you have learned.

National
Rose Month

National
Safety Month

National
Candy Month

Turkey Lovers'
Month

June

Wish Superman a happy birthday! The first issue of the comic book *Superman* was published June 1, 1938.

▶ What does the prefix super- mean? Think of some words, besides Superman, that have the prefix.

▶ Of the following superhuman powers, which would you most want? Why?

x-ray vision
ability to fly
ability to run fast
superhuman strength

▶ Superman stories have taken many forms besides comic books. Name several other kinds.

Happy Birthday
S

Champion swimmer Johnny Weissmuller was born in 1904. He won five Olympic gold medals and set 67 world records in swimming. Then he became a motion picture actor. His most famous role was Tarzan.

▶ Swimmers use specific meanings for words that tell about their sport. Give the swimming meaning for each of the following words:

stroke   block   starter
finish   lane

▶ What characteristics would a champion swimmer have? Which ones do you think would also be important to a motion picture actor?

▶ Find out which world records Johnny Weissmuller set.

In 1965, 120 miles above Earth, Major Edward H. White II opened the hatch of *Gemini 4* and stepped out of the space capsule, becoming the first U.S. astronaut to walk in space. Major White remained outside the capsule for just over 20 minutes.

▶ Astronaut White opened the hatch. What is a hatch? What other words have a similar meaning?

▶ How do you think you would feel if you were the first to do something?

▶ Learn more about the Gemini space flights.

In France in 1070 a new cheese was made. Aged in the caves for over three months before it was eaten, the cheese was called "Roquefort" after a nearby town.

▶ What does it mean to age something? What things do you know that are aged?

▶ What is your favorite kind of cheese? Describe its flavor.

▶ Find out how cheese is made. Does the length of time that a cheese is aged vary?

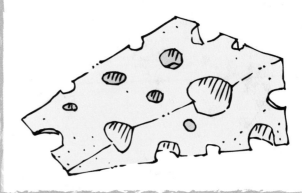

Today is World Environment Day. Since 1972 people all over the world have used today as a special time to recognize their concern for the earth.

▶ What is an environment? Describe your environment.

▶ What things can you do to improve your environment and reduce pollution?

▶ Find out what your local community is doing to protect your environment.

In 1933 the first U.S. drive-in movie opened in Camden, New Jersey. The huge screen measured 40 feet by 50 feet and could be easily seen by everyone who sat in cars to watch the movie. Admission was 25 cents per person plus 25 cents for the car.

▶ As the number of automobiles increase, compound words using the word drive are used more often. Write as many of these words as you can think of.

▶ Have you ever been to a drive-in movie? What other types of drive-in businesses are you familiar with?

▶ Compare the size of the drive-in movie screen with a regular movie screen, a television screen, and a computer screen.

In 1769 frontiersman Daniel Boone first saw the forests and woodlands of the area that would become the state of Kentucky. The Kentucky Historical Society has declared June 7 "Boone Day."

▶ What is a frontier? What does that tell you about what the word frontiersman means?

▶ What do you think would be the most exciting thing about exploring the frontier? What dangers would there be?

▶ Daniel Boone is credited with opening the Wilderness Road, the primary route to the West following the French and Indian War. Find out more about the Wilderness Road and its place in American history.

Architect Frank Lloyd Wright was born on June 8, 1869. Mr. Wright believed that buildings should go with their surroundings. One of his most famous houses, Falling Water, has trees growing through the roof, large rocks sticking up through the floor, and a stream running underneath.

▶ What is an architect?

▶ If you were going to design a house, what things do you think would be important to consider?

▶ Find out more about the houses, buildings, and furniture that Frank Lloyd Wright designed.

9

Happy Birthday, Michael J. Fox! This television and movie star was born in Alberta, Canada, on June 9, 1961. In 1991 he was diagnosed with Parkinson's disease. He has retired from show business to promote scientific research that will someday prevent and cure the disease.

▶ What adjectives would you use to describe a star?

▶ The word star is used to describe outstanding performers. Who do you know that could be called a star? Tell why.

▶ Learn more about Parkinson's disease.

10

Maurice Sendak was born on June 10, 1928. He was often sick as a child. He didn't like school and he wasn't good at sports, but he loved to read. When he graduated from high school, he went to art school at night. He combined his love for books and his art to become an author and illustrator.

▶ What is an artist? Do all artists draw pictures or paint?

▶ Because Maurice Sendak's mother worried about him as a child, he draws the moon peeking in to check on the characters in many of his picture book stories. Name all the people who worry about you and watch over you to keep you from harm.

▶ Read several of Sendak's books. What awards has he won?

11

Jacques Cousteau, French naval officer, marine explorer, author, and documentary filmmaker, was born in 1910. He helped to perfect the Aqualung,™ which enabled divers to stay underwater for several hours.

- ▶ *Aqua* means "water." Think of words you know that have aqua in them.

- ▶ Have you ever dived underwater? As a marine explorer, what things might you see?

- ▶ Jacques Cousteau sailed aboard his ship, the *Calypso*. Find out more about the *Calypso* and her voyages.

Anne Frank was born on June 12, 1929. Because she and her family were Jewish, they spent 25 months hidden in an attic above her father's office during World War II. Her diary about these years was saved and published after her death.

- ▶ What is a *diary*? What kinds of things could you write in a diary?

- ▶ What problems do you think would occur if you had to remain in one place for two years?

- ▶ Anne Frank was one of over 1,000,000 Jewish children under the age of 16 who died during the Holocaust. Read a part of her diary and learn more about her experience.

Good-bye, *Pioneer 10*. After more than 10 years in space, *Pioneer 10*, the world's first outer-planetary probe, left the solar system in 1983. It was headed in the direction of the star Ross 246.

▶ What does solar mean? What is a solar system?

▶ What kinds of things do you think exist in outer space? Are there other forms of life?

▶ Before leaving the solar system, *Pioneer 10* sent back the first close-up pictures of Jupiter. Find copies of those pictures. What can you learn about Jupiter by looking at them?

14

Today is Flag Day in the United States. In 1777 the Continental Congress decided to use the Stars and Stripes flag as the national flag of the United States.

▶ When you pledge allegiance to the flag, what are you doing? What does pledge mean? What does allegiance mean?

▶ If you had been Betsy Ross, what would your flag design have looked like?

▶ Find out more about the history of your country's flag.

15

It's Flag Day in Denmark. Legend has it that on the night of June 15, 1219, the Danish army was caught by a surprise attack. In answer to prayers, a crack of thunder sounded and a red flag with a white cross fell from heaven. When King Valdemar raised the flag, his troops won the battle.

▶ What is a legend?

▶ How do you think legends develop? Do you know any legends about how something came into existence?

▶ Choose another country. Find out what its flag looks like. Is there a legend associated with the flag?

16

At the first World's Fair in 1893, F. W. Rueckheim introduced a new snack made with popcorn, peanuts, and molasses. Three years later Mr. Rueckheim and his brother marketed the snack as Cracker Jack®.

▶ What would you say if you took a bite of a new snack and you liked it? What if you didn't like it?

▶ When a salesman first tasted the snack he said, "That's a crack jack!" So the Rueckheims named the snack Cracker Jack. Use your responses to a new snack to name the snack.

▶ Find out how your favorite snack got its name.

17

In 1950 the first kidney transplant was performed in Chicago. The operation was performed by Dr. Lawler.

▶ What does its mean to transplant something? What is a kidney transplant?

▶ Why might it be necessary to transplant an organ like a kidney? What are the advantages and disadvantages?

▶ Learn more about other organ transplants.

June 18 is International Picnic Day!

▶ Describe a picnic for someone who has never been to one.

▶ What makes a picnic different from any other meal? What are your favorite picnic foods?

▶ Look in a cookbook and find a recipe for a good picnic food. Tell why you think the food would be good for a picnic.

19

The Statue of Liberty arrived in New York Harbor in 1885. It was a gift from the people of France to the people of the United States. It stands more than 300 feet high and symbolizes freedom and democracy to the United States and to the world.

▶ What are some other words that mean the same thing as liberty?

▶ What does liberty mean to you? Do you feel you have liberty? Has there been a time in your life when you felt you didn't have the liberty you wanted? When?

▶ A famous poem is inscribed on the base of the Statue of Liberty. Find the poem and read it.

20

Today in 1782 the Congress of the United States declared the bald eagle as the nation's official symbol.

▶ What is a symbol? What other symbols can you identify?

▶ Do you think the bald eagle is an appropriate symbol for the U.S.? Why or why not? What other animal might be a good symbol for the U.S.? Why?

▶ Choose another country. What is the symbol of that country? Why was the symbol chosen?

Prince William of England was born on June 21, 1982. He is the son of Prince Charles and the late Princess Diana. It is likely that he will one day become King William V.

▶ The son of a king or queen is addressed as a prince. Name other royal terms of address. Tell what they mean.

▶ Would you like to be a prince or a princess? Tell why or why not.

▶ Name three other countries that have royal families and list the ruling members of the families.

Today is Doughnuts Day. Doughnuts were "invented" in 1847.

▶ How would you describe a doughnut?

▶ There are many different kinds of doughnuts. Name as many as you can.

▶ How are doughnuts made?

23

Johannes Gutenberg, the German inventor of the printing press, was born today. He is considered one of the most influential people in history. Gutenberg's printing press allowed printers to mass-produce documents and, eventually, books.

▶ What does influential mean?

▶ How does a printing press affect your life? Do you think that it was one of the most important inventions ever made?

▶ Gutenberg was working as a goldsmith when he invented the printing press. What is a goldsmith? Did Gutenberg invent anything else?

24

Today is St. John's Day, named in honor of St. John the Baptist. In Spain, men and boys named *John* receive cakes made in the shape of a J. Norwegians light bonfires along the fjords. People in Quebec, Canada, celebrate with parades, bonfires, and street dancing.

▶ There are many different words, such as holiday, that include the word day. Name as many as you can.

▶ If you celebrated a name-day for people with your name, what kind of a celebration would you want to have?

▶ The name *John* has many different variations. Find as many as you can.

In 1993 Canada's first woman prime minister took office. The Right Honorable A. Kim Campbell held office for just four months before her party was defeated in a general election.

▶ What does it mean to be defeated? Give a synonym.

▶ The way you address people is sometimes determined by the position they hold. How do you address the leader of your country? State or province? Principal? Teacher? Religious leader? Dentist?

▶ Choose a famous woman leader. Tell about her accomplishments. Do you think she is or was a good leader? Justify your answer.

Babe Didrikson Zaharias was born on June 26, 1911. She was one of the greatest woman athletes of all time. She set world records in the hurdles, javelin throw, high jump, and baseball throw. She also played baseball, tennis, and basketball. She won 17 golf tournaments in a row.

▶ What is a javelin? Compare a javelin and a baseball. Tell how they are alike and different.

▶ What makes a good athlete? Do the same attributes help in every sport?

▶ Choose another famous athlete. Find out about the person's life and the athletic records he or she set.

94

The British Parliament began with the signing of the Magna Carta on June 27, 1215. King John was forced to sign the document that gave the English people certain rights. The Parliament consists of the House of Lords and the House of Commons.

▶ What is a document? Have you ever signed a document?

▶ When a bill becomes a law in England, it must have royal assent. That means the King or Queen must approve it. Do you think this is a good idea? Why or why not?

▶ Learn more about the Magna Carta.

The first dog show was held in 1859 in England.

▶ Describe how you would teach a dog a trick.

▶ Which animal do you think is smarter—a dog or a cat? Why?

▶ Find out about the different kinds of dog shows. Are there dog shows in your area?

First Prize

In 1953 the U.S. Interstate Highway System was born. The Federal Highway Act authorized the construction of 42,500 miles of freeway from coast to coast.

▶ What does interstate mean? What other words do you know with the prefix inter-?

▶ Why is a good system of roadways important to a country?

▶ Using an atlas, trace a route from coast to coast on U.S. interstate freeways.

Have you ever eaten a Twinkie®? They were created in Chicago in 1930. Their creator, James A. Dewar, died on June 30, 1985.

▶ *Twinkie* is an example of a word that was made up to name a new product. Tell what these "new" words name.

  Skittles®

  Smoothie®

  Slurpee®

  McNugget®

▶ Do you think the name of a product is important? Why or why not?

▶ Imagine a new snack. Describe it and make up a name for it.

National Foreign Language Month

National Hot Dog Month

National Blueberry Month

National Recreation and Parks Month

JULY

What Happened Today? • EMC 1015

1

Wave the flag! March in a parade! Today is Canada Day. On July 1, 1867, the British North America Act united the provinces of Canada in a British dominion. Canada became a self-governing, autonomous part of the British Commonwealth.

▶ Describe a parade. List all the different verbs that tell how people move in a parade.

▶ The word autonomous means independent and self-governing. Can you think of ways in which you are autonomous?

▶ What other countries are part of the British Commonwealth?

2

In 1865 William and Catherine Booth founded the Salvation Army. They worked with a small group of homeless people in the slums of London. Today over 9,000 Salvation Army centers provide food, shelter, and training to help others around the world.

▶ What is an army? What does an army do? How is the Salvation Army different from most armies?

▶ Have you ever "fought" for something? Can groups "fight" in a positive way? Explain.

▶ Contact your local Salvation Army. Find out what it is doing in your community.

The song-and-dance man George M. Cohan was born July 3, 1878, in Providence, Rhode Island. George appeared on stage for the first time when he was nine years old. He became a famous playwright and composer, as well as an actor.

▶ What do you think a song-and-dance man does? What is a playwright? How is a playwright different from an author?

▶ Mr. Cohan is remembered for his 1904 role as a Yankee Doodle boy. Who is Yankee Doodle? What do you think a Yankee Doodle boy would be like?

▶ Find the words to one of Mr. Cohan's songs, such as "I'm a Yankee Doodle Dandy," "It's a Grand Old Flag," or "Give My Regards to Broadway." What do the songs tell you about Mr. Cohan and his feelings about his country?

July 4 is Independence Day in the United States. In 1776 the Declaration of Independence was adopted by the Continental Congress. The Declaration of Independence guaranteed U.S. citizens certain rights—the rights of "life, liberty, and the pursuit of happiness."

▶ What does liberty mean? What does pursuit mean?

▶ Name some of the things that make you happy.

▶ Learn more about the signing of the Declaration of Independence. Read the document. Think about what it means to U.S. citizens today.

5

How about a bicycle race? In 1903 Henri Desgrange, an editor of a daily sports newspaper, started the Tour de France. Today thousands of cyclists from around the world ride the 2,500-mile (4,000-km) course that circles France.

► What is a cyclist? Name all of the things a cyclist might ride.

► If you were going to complete a three-week race, what kind of preparations would you have to make? Do you think you could do a three-week race?

► Find the route of the Tour de France for the previous year. Who was the winner? What was the winning time?

6

American patriot Nathan Hale was born on July 6, 1755. Educated at Yale, Hale was a teacher until the Revolutionary War began. He volunteered to go behind enemy lines and report on troop movements. He was caught and hung.

► What is a patriot?

► In addition to Nathan Hale, who do you think is a patriot? Tell why.

► Nathan Hale's final words were, "I only regret that I have but one life to lose for my country." Find another patriotic quotation. Tell who said it and on what occasion.

In 1976, for the first time in history, women were enrolled in the United States Military Academy at West Point, New York. The U.S. Military Academy was founded by Congress in 1802 to educate and train young men. In 1980, 62 female cadets graduated.

▶ What does it mean to enroll? Have you ever enrolled in something?

▶ Colleges and academies that admit both men and women are called coeducational. Do you think that women and men should be allowed to attend the same schools? Why or why not?

▶ Choose a college or an academy. Find out when it was founded and if it is coeducational.

On July 8, 1776, in Philadelphia, Pennsylvania, the Liberty Bell rang out. It summoned citizens to the first public reading of the Declaration of Independence. Words on the side of the bell read "Proclaim liberty throughout all the land...."

▶ What does it mean to summon someone? Tell about a time you were summoned.

▶ Bells are rung to signal many different things. Name as many as you can.

▶ Learn more about the Liberty Bell. It has a famous flaw. What is it?

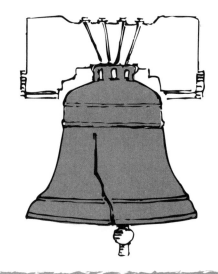

Elias Howe was born in 1819 in Massachusetts. Mr. Howe invented the lockstitch sewing machine. The machine used two threads to sew a straight, durable seam.

▶ What does durable mean? Why is it important that a seam be durable?

▶ Mr. Howe's machine sewed as fast as five workers sewing by hand. Do you think that the workers were happy about the invention? Why or why not?

▶ There are many sewing-related expressions. Choose one and explain its meaning.

on pins and needles

like trying to find a needle in a haystack

a stitch in time saves nine

Happy Birthday, Arthur Ashe! Arthur was the first African-American man to win a major tennis tournament. He began playing tennis as a skinny 10-year-old and went on to be ranked number one in the world.

▶ What does it mean to be ranked? Name some things that are ranked.

▶ Arthur Ashe competed in tennis tournaments. Have you ever competed in a tournament? Can you compete in other ways?

▶ Learn more about Arthur Ashe's life.

Charlotte and Wilbur would wish E. B. White best wishes today. Mr. White was born in 1899 in New York. Charlotte, a wise spider, and Wilbur, a young pig, are two characters from his book *Charlotte's Web*. The two were modeled after animals on Mr. White's farm.

▶ Charlotte wove terrific and amazing into her web above Wilbur's pen. Think of some other synonyms she might have used for these words.

▶ E. B. White's stories have been made into movies. Do you like movies or books better? Tell why?

▶ E. B. White used personification. (His animals took on human characteristics.) Choose an animal character. Give examples of how the animal was personified.

In 1859 William Goodale patented a paper bag manufacturing machine.

▶ A paper bag is one type of container. What is a container? Name other kinds of containers.

▶ Paper bags can be used for many purposes. Name as many as you can.

▶ Establish a paper bag collection. Think of the different categories of bags and organize your collection. Visit the Web site of a paper bag distributor. Compare your categories you named with those of the distributor.

13

Henry Rowe Schoolcraft, led by an Ojibwe guide, discovered the source of the Mississippi River. According to Schoolcraft, the mighty river begins at Lake Itasca and travels 2,500 miles to the Gulf of Mexico.

▶ What is a source?

▶ What is a guide? Why did explorers use guides? Where would you be able to act as a guide?

▶ Learn more about the Mississippi River.

14

In 1789 crowds in Paris stormed a prison named the Bastille. They freed the prisoners and carried them through the streets. This began the French Revolution, when the people rebelled against the king. Today French citizens celebrate their Independence Day with parades, fireworks, and street dances.

▶ What does stormed mean?

▶ Revolutions have occurred in many countries. What makes a revolution? What revolutions are occurring today?

▶ Many famous people have spent time in prison. Learn more about a famous prison or prisoner.

15

Today is Saint Swithin's Day. An old English belief or superstition says that if it rains today, it will rain for the next 40 days.

▶ What is a superstition?

▶ If you had the choice of living where it rained every day or where it never rained, which would you choose? Why?

▶ Learn about another weather superstition.

16

In 1935 Oklahoma City, Oklahoma, installed the first parking meters.

▶ What is a meter? What meters do you use?

▶ Why do you suppose a city would install parking meters? Do you think having parking meters is good? Why or why not?

▶ Do a survey of parking in your area. Do cars park on the street or in lots? How many cars does each lot hold? Is there a charge for parking?

Disneyland opened in Anaheim, California, on July 17, 1955. Walt Disney wanted to create a place where his employees and their families could relax. His ideas multiplied. The 160-acre park opened with five different "lands," with rivers, waterfalls, and mountains.

▶ Would you like to be an employee at Disneyland? Why or why not?

▶ Disneyland includes flying elephants, spinning teacups, and bobsleds speeding down a mountain. If you could design a new attraction for Disneyland, what would it be?

▶ How has Disneyland changed since its opening in 1955? Document some of the changes.

John Paul Jones died on July 18, 1792. He was a naval hero of the American Revolution. In the heat of battle, British ships demanded he surrender his fleet. He responded, "I have not yet begun to fight." John Paul Jones eventually won the battle.

▶ What does it mean to surrender? Did John Paul Jones surrender?

▶ Born in Scotland, John Paul Jones went to sea when he was 12 years old. He worked as a cabin boy. What do you think a cabin boy would do? Would you like to be one?

▶ Learn more about the U.S. Navy during the American Revolution. What were some of the famous battles?

In 1869 John Muir wrote the first entry in a four-month journal account of his trip to Yosemite Valley in the Sierra Nevada. Muir described the mountains, plants, and animals that he saw each day. He became one of the first to advocate forestry conservation.

▶ What is a journal? Have you ever kept a journal?

▶ What kinds of things might John Muir have seen on a trip to the Sierras? Have you ever taken a trip to a mountain forest? What did you see?

▶ Where are the Sierras? Learn more about John Muir and his career as a naturalist.

On July 20, 1969, Astronauts Neil Armstrong and Edwin (Buzz) Aldrin became the first men to walk on the moon. They returned to Earth with photos and moon rocks.

▶ Describe how you think it must have felt to be the first person to step onto the moon.

▶ Describe how the moon looks in the night sky from Earth. Now imagine that you are standing on the moon. When you look at the sky, how has your view changed?

▶ Find out what Armstrong said when he stepped out of the lunar module *Eagle* onto the moon. What do you think he meant?

21

The Aswan High Dam was completed in Egypt on July 21, 1970. The dam's 12 giant turbines were designed to provide enough power to make Egypt self-sufficient. By controlling the waters of the Nile, the dam also protects Egypt against drought and flooding.

▶ What does it mean to be self-sufficient? Are you self-sufficient?

▶ When the flow of a river is changed, the effects can be both good and bad. Make a list of things you think might happen.

▶ Find out more about the Aswan High Dam. What have been its good and bad effects?

22

One legend says that on July 22, 1284, a strange man arrived in a small German village and made a deal with the townspeople to get rid of the rats in the town. He played his pipe and the rats followed him straight into the river. History remembers this man as the Pied Piper of Hamelin. (Historians debate the actual date the piper arrived in Hamelin.)

▶ What is a legend? Are legends always true?

▶ When the townspeople of Hamelin did not live up to their part of the deal, the piper played his pipe again, and this time the town's children followed him out of town. Do you think the piper was justified in taking the town's children? Why or why not?

▶ Locate Hamelin in an atlas. What river is close to the city?

23

In 1904, at the St. Louis World's Fair, a baker rolled up some pastry into cones and sold them to an ice-cream vendor who was running out of dishes. Visitors at the World's Fair loved the cold treats!

▶ What is a vendor? Do you have vendors in your community?

▶ The ice-cream cone was a tasty invention. Think of a new way to eat ice cream.

▶ The 1904 St. Louis World's Fair included many exciting exhibits. Find out more about the fair and some of the innovations that were "big news" at the time.

24

It was 1824. The presidential election was approaching. Who would be elected? The first public opinion poll was conducted in Wilmington, Delaware, to answer that question.

▶ What is a poll? What do you do when you give an opinion?

▶ Have you ever participated in a poll? Do you think a poll provides valuable information? Why or why not?

▶ Conduct a classroom opinion poll using one of the following questions:

Should the school day be longer, shorter, or the same length?

Should homework be eliminated?

Should the class be arranged in rows or groups?

Chicago Bears' Hall of Fame running back Walter Payton was born on July 25, 1954. "Sweetness" was known for his high-stepping sideline runs and his 100% effort. At the time of his death in 1999, he was the all-time leading rusher.

► The game of football has a vocabulary of its own. Explain what a rusher does. What is a sideline run?

► Why do you think Walter Payton had the nickname Sweetness? Is it a nickname you would expect a professional football player to have? Why or why not?

► Choose another professional football player and learn about his life.

In 1775 Benjamin Franklin established the United States Postal Service.

► When you mail a letter, you seal the envelope and put a stamp on it. What other meanings do the words letter, seal, and stamp have?

► Do you think a postal service is important? Why or why not?

► Visit a post office or the U.S. Postal Service Web site and find out what things can be sent in the mail and what things cannot be sent. Why are there regulations about what can and can't be sent?

President of the United States of America
1600 Pennsylvania Avenue
Washington, D.C.

Mr. Samuel Uchida
100 Main Street
Hometown

27

American writer and art connoisseur Gertrude Stein died in France on July 27, 1946. Although she went to school in the United States, Ms. Stein lived in Paris. Her home was a gathering place for famous artists and writers, such as Picasso, Matisse, and Hemingway.

► What is a connoisseur? Do you know anyone who is a connoisseur?

► If you could invite several famous people to visit your home, who would you invite? Why?

► Gertrude Stein was a mentor to young artists. Learn more about what it means to be a mentor. Find someone who is a mentor in your community and interview that person.

28

Happy Birthday, Beatrix Potter! Born in London in 1866, Beatrix created her famous character Peter Rabbit to cheer up a sick five-year-old friend. Her animal stories and drawings have been children's favorites ever since.

► What is a character?

► As a child, Beatrix sometimes smuggled animals into her room. Have you ever had a similar experience? Tell about it.

► Beatrix Potter wrote about many different animals. Make a list of the characters in her books.

In 1715 a hurricane sunk 10 Spanish treasure galleons off the coast of what is now Florida.

▶ What is a galleon? Can you name some other kinds of ships?

▶ What kind of treasure do you think the galleons were carrying?

▶ Learn more about shipwrecks. Choose one. Give the ship's name, its cargo, the location of the wreck, and whether it has been recovered.

Dr. Douglas Engelbart was born in 1925. Who is Dr. Engelbart? A computer visionary, he created and patented the computer mouse.

▶ What is a visionary?

▶ During the 1950s, Dr. Engelbart believed that computers would help people in their everyday lives. Was his vision correct? Support your answer with specific examples.

▶ Learn more about the development of computers.

In 1928, MGM's trademark lion roared for the first time as it introduced the motion picture studio's first talking picture. The only spoken word in the film was "Hello."

▶ What is a trademark? What trademarks do you recognize?

▶ Why do you think companies have trademarks? Do you think they are beneficial? Why or why not?

▶ Choose a familiar trademark. Discover when it was first used and why.

Children's Vision and Learning Month

Don't Wait-Celebrate! Week (second week)

National Inventor's Month

National Back-to-School Month

August

Fashion designer Yves Saint Laurent was born in Oran, Algeria, on August 1, 1936. At the age of 17, he arrived in Paris with a book of sketches. His designs have influenced fashion ever since. He is credited with making women's trousers popular for any occasion.

► What is a designer? A fashion designer?

► If you could change what you wear, what changes would you make? Why?

► Choose a period in history. Look at the popular fashions. Compare them with current fashion trends.

Pierre Charles L'Enfant was born in 1754 in Paris, France. After serving as an officer in the Revolutionary War, L'Enfant was selected by Washington and Jefferson to draw up plans for a new national capital at Washington, D.C. L'Enfant's plan featured broad avenues radiating out from the capitol building.

► What does the word radiating mean? Name some things that radiate from a center.

► What are the advantages of designing an entire city before construction is begun? What are the disadvantages?

► Find a map of Washington, D.C., today. Compare it with a drawing of L'Enfant's plan.

Christopher Columbus set sail from Spain in 1492. He left Palos, Spain, half an hour before sunrise with three ships and a crew of 90 men.

▶ What does it mean to set sail?

▶ Christopher Columbus is known as Admiral of the Ocean Sea. Do you think this is a good name for him? Explain why or why not.

▶ Learn more about Columbus's first voyage. Which country did Columbus hope to reach? How do you think he felt as he began his journey?

The U.S. Coast Guard was founded in 1790. The men and women of the Coast Guard have as their motto *Semper Paratus*, which means "Always Ready."

▶ What is a motto? Does your school have one?

▶ What kinds of things do you think a coast guard would do? Visit the U.S. Coast Guard Web site, or read to discover whether your ideas are correct.

▶ Search and rescue is a job that the Coast Guard shares with other organizations. Find out what organization in your community is responsible for search and rescue operations.

In 1583 Sir Humphrey Gilbert, aboard his sailing ship *The Squirrel,* sighted the Newfoundland coast. He claimed the area around St. John's Harbor in the name of the queen. This was the first English colony established in North America.

▶ What does it mean to claim an area in the name of the queen?

▶ Sir Humphrey Gilbert was lost at sea on his return trip to England. What dangers face ocean explorers today? Were those dangers greater in 1583? Explain why or why not.

▶ What colonies exist today? Learn more about a colony of your choice.

Sixteen-year-old Gertrude Ederle swam the English Channel on August 6, 1926. She was the first woman to complete the swim. It took her 14 hours and 31 minutes.

▶ What is a channel? What other meanings do you know for this word?

▶ What problems would a swimmer encounter in a 14-hour swim? How could these problems be solved?

▶ Find the route of Gertrude Ederle's swim. How did she solve the problems of a long ocean swim?

 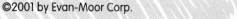

In 1959 the U.S. satellite *Explorer VI* transmitted the first picture of Earth from space. For the first time, scientists had a likeness of the planet based on more than projections and conjectures.

▶ What do the words projections and conjectures mean? Have you ever made a projection?

▶ Why was this picture from space so important?

▶ Current views of Earth from orbiting satellites are available online and in reference books. Find one and compare it with a globe or map.

Odie, a flop-eared pup with huge eyes, first appeared in the *Garfield* comic strip on August 8, 1978. He is Garfield's sidekick.

▶ What is a sidekick?

▶ Odie, a dog, and Garfield, a cat, are unlikely sidekicks. Why do you think the creators of this comic strip paired a cat and a dog? Do you think it was a good idea? Why or why not?

▶ Find another comic strip. Describe one of the characters in the strip.

In 1944 the Forest Service created Smokey the Bear to represent forest fire prevention.

▶ Name ways to prevent forest fires.

▶ Why do you think they chose a bear as a symbol? What other forest animals might they have named?

▶ Smokey was named after a real survivor of a forest fire. Find the details about this special bear.

The Smithsonian Institution was founded on August 10, 1846. This set of museums was designed to hold the many scientific, historical, and cultural collections that belong to the United States.

▶ What is a museum? What might you find in one?

▶ The Smithsonian Institute is located in Washington, D.C. Do you think that is a good location? Why or why not?

▶ What museums are included in the Smithsonian? Choose one and find out what exhibits you might view in it.

The largest shopping mall in America, Mall of America, opened in Bloomington, Minnesota, in 1992.

▶ What is a mall?

▶ Name 10 kinds of stores you might find in a mall. What else would you find at a mall in addition to stores?

▶ Visit a mall (in person or online). Draw a map of the mall, including all the different things you saw.

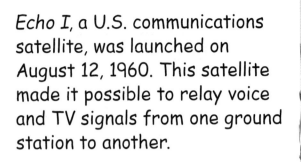

Echo I, a U.S. communications satellite, was launched on August 12, 1960. This satellite made it possible to relay voice and TV signals from one ground station to another.

▶ What is a **satellite**? How is a satellite launched?

▶ Why is it good to be able to relay voice and TV signals in space?

▶ Make a list of ways that you communicate. Choose one and find out more about its history.

Today is International Left-Handers Day.

▶ What does it mean to be left-handed? What do the following "left" expressions mean?

leftovers
left-handed compliment
out in left field

▶ Take a classroom poll. How many students are left-handed? How many are right-handed? Of the left-handed students, how many do some things with their right hand?

▶ Switch to your opposite hand for all activities for half an hour. What difficulties did the switch create?

In 1240 in Genoa, Italy, Count Fieschi of Lavagna surprised guests at his wedding with a cake over 30 feet tall. He served the cake to all the people in the town. On August 14, people of Genoa still enjoy Fieschi's Cake.

▶ Measure 30 feet. Find something that is about 30 feet tall.

▶ What is your favorite kind of cake? If you were planning a three-tier wedding cake, what flavor would you make each tier?

▶ A single eight-inch tall layer serves 20 people. The stands between layers are four inches tall. The flowers on top are four inches tall. How many people will a cake 30 feet tall serve?

In 1848 M. Waldo Hanchett patented the dental chair.

- ▶ Describe the dental chair your dentist uses.

- ▶ Would you rather go to the dentist or the doctor? Why?

- ▶ Choose a chair invented for a special purpose. Describe the special features of the chair and find out who patented it.

In the Klondike region of the Yukon, at Bonanza Creek, George Washington Carmack discovered gold on August 16 or 17, 1896. During the following year more than 30,000 people joined the gold rush to the area.

- ▶ What is a bonanza?

- ▶ Why do you think the name of the creek near George Carmack's discovery was changed from Rabbit Creek to Bonanza Creek? Do you think this was a good change? Tell why or why not.

- ▶ Find out more about the Yukon gold rush.

In 1978 three Americans became the first people to complete a transatlantic trip in a balloon. They traveled 3,200 miles in 137 hours, 18 minutes.

- ▶ What does transatlantic mean? List other words that you know with the trans- prefix. Give their meanings.

- ▶ What would it be like to travel in a balloon? Do you think you would like it? Tell why or why not.

- ▶ Find out about the *Double Eagle II*, the craft used in this first transatlantic crossing.

The first mail-order catalog was published by Montgomery Ward on August 18, 1872. It was a single sheet of paper.

- ▶ What is a mail-order catalog?

- ▶ Have you ever ordered from a catalog? What kind of things did you order? What are the advantages and disadvantages of ordering from a catalog?

- ▶ Choose a mail-order catalog. Look through it. Practice filling out an order form as if you were ordering something.

Today is National Aviation Day in the United States. It has been observed annually since 1939.

▶ What does aviation mean?

▶ List all the different kinds of planes that you can.

▶ Find out how airplanes today are different from those flown in 1939. Which planes would you rather fly in? Explain why.

AUGUST
20

Benjamin Harrison, the 23rd president of the United States, was born on August 20, 1833. He was the grandson of William Henry Harrison, the 9th president of the United States.

▶ Benjamin Harrison was preceded in office by Grover Cleveland. What does **preceded** mean? He was succeeded in office by Grover Cleveland. What does **succeeded** mean?

▶ Have you done something that one of your relatives did before you? Tell about what it was.

▶ Find out which other U.S. presidents were related.

21

In 1973 the first house made of recycled products was built in Richmond, Virginia.

▶ What does the phrase "reduce, reuse, recycle" mean to you?

▶ Why is it important to recycle?

▶ Locate something made of recycled materials in your classroom or community.

22

William Sheppard patented a liquid form of soap in 1865.

▶ What is a liquid? List all the other liquids you can think of.

▶ Describe, step by step, how to wash your hands using liquid soap.

▶ Choose something that is made in both solid and liquid forms. Describe the advantages and disadvantages of each form.

In 1975 Tony Flor did 7,351 consecutive loop-the-loops with a yo-yo.

▶ What does consecutive mean?

▶ Describe a yo-yo and explain how to use one. Have you ever used a yo-yo?

▶ Learn a yo-yo trick and demonstrate it.

In 1869 Cornelius Swarthout patented the waffle iron.

▶ What are other meanings for the word iron?

▶ Which do you prefer, waffles or pancakes? Why?

▶ Find a recipe for making waffles.

The movie *The Wizard of Oz* was first released on August 25, 1939. Dorothy, a Kansas farm girl, and her dog Toto are swept into a tornado and land in a place inhabited by little people called Munchkins. The movie tells about their attempts to get back to Kansas.

▶ What is a tornado? Is it possible for a tornado to lift a house from one spot and move it to another?

▶ Dorothy follows a yellow brick road to the Emerald City of Oz. Do you think making a yellow brick road to a specific location is a good way to simplify directions? Tell why or why not.

▶ Read all or part of *The Wizard of Oz*. Describe one of the characters in detail.

On August 26, 1883, the eruption of the Indonesian volcanic island Krakatoa was heard 3,000 miles away. It was the biggest explosion in history.

▶ What is a volcanic island? What other words do you know that mean explosion?

▶ What would you do to protect yourself from a volcanic eruption?

▶ Indonesia is a nation made up of many islands. Locate it on the map. Find the island of Krakatoa.

In 1859 W. A. Smith discovered oil in a water shaft being sunk in western Pennsylvania. Smith saw a dark film floating on the water. Soon thereafter, 20 barrels of crude oil were being pumped each day.

▶ What is a shaft? What does film mean in the phrase "dark film floating on the water"?

▶ Have you ever found one thing when you were looking for another thing? Tell about your discovery.

▶ At first, oil was refined into kerosene and used for lighting. How is oil used today?

On August 28, 1999, the *Mir* space station was abandoned by its last crew. The space station had been launched in 1986. It had been aloft for about 5,000 days and had orbited the earth more than 77,000 times.

▶ Name things that are aloft. Tell what aloft means.

▶ Nearly 100 people had spent some time on *Mir*. What kinds of things do you think they were able to learn?

▶ Find a diagram of the *Mir* space station. What are the living quarters like?

Chop suey was first introduced in New York City in 1896. It was prepared by a Chinese cook for a dinner attended by the Chinese ambassador Li-Hung Chang and the American president Grover Cleveland.

▶ Chop suey includes many different ingredients. What are ingredients? Find a recipe for chop suey and list its ingredients.

▶ Some people use chopsticks to eat chop suey and some people use forks. What are the differences between chopsticks and forks? Which do you think would be easier to use?

▶ Choose a food that you like to eat. Try to find out where the dish originated.

Author and illustrator Donald Crews was born on August 30, 1938. His Caldecott Honor book *Freight Train* describes memories of summer train rides to his grandmother's house. He uses bright colors and basic shapes to illustrate his simple text.

▶ What is text? What other words do you use for text?

▶ Do you have a memory of a special experience that you could make into a story? Tell about the experience.

▶ Donald Crews enjoys tricking his readers by using illustrations from one book in another book. Can you find the same picture in two of his books?

31

Kyrgyzstan, Trinidad and Tobago, and Malaysia celebrate independence today. In 1991 Kyrgyzstan declared independence from what was then the Soviet Union. Trinidad and Tobago became nations within the British Commonwealth in 1962. Malaysia became independent from Britain in 1957.

▸ Each of these countries has declared August 31 a national holiday. What is a national holiday?

▸ Many countries become independent from other countries. Why do you think this happens?

▸ Choose another country. Find out when it celebrates its Independence Day. Tell about the type of celebration that it has.

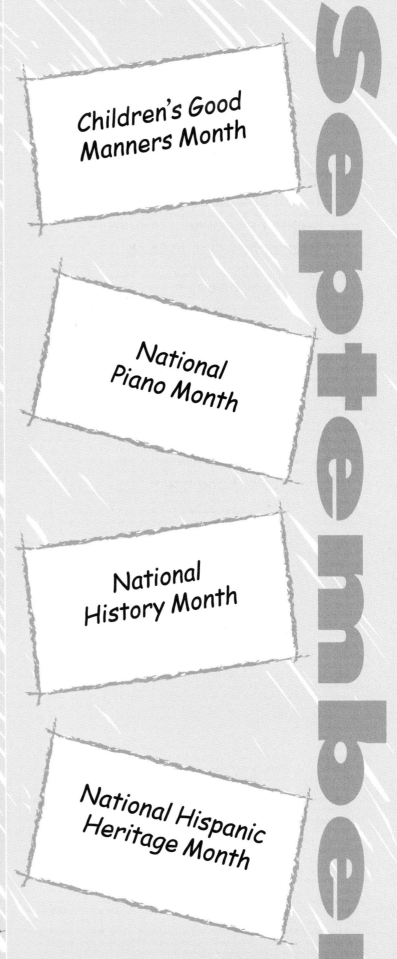

Children's Good Manners Month

National Piano Month

National History Month

National Hispanic Heritage Month

September

What Happened Today? • EMC 1015

Today is Emma M. Nutt Day in honor of the first woman telephone operator. She began her career in Boston, Massachusetts, in 1878.

▶ What does a telephone operator do?

▶ What job do you think is the most difficult? the easiest? the most exciting? the dullest? Why?

▶ How has the job of telephone operator changed over the years?

On September 2, 490 B.C., a runner was sent from Marathon to Sparta in Greece to seek help for Athenians fighting in the Persian Wars. The distance between the two towns was 26 miles.

▶ Have you ever heard the term marathon? What does it mean? Explain how this meaning came to be.

▶ According to the legend, Phidippides actually ran the distance between the two towns three times carrying messages back and forth. Do you think the legend is true? Why or why not?

▶ This story describes the origin of an athletic event, the marathon run. Choose an athletic event. Find out how it began.

3

On September 3, 1838, a slave named Frederick Douglass escaped to freedom. He dressed as a sailor and boarded a train in Baltimore, Maryland. He rode to Wilmington, Delaware, where he caught a steamboat to the free city of Philadelphia and then went on to New York City.

▶ Frederick Douglass became a great orator and one of the leaders of the antislavery struggle in the United States. What is an orator?

▶ Have you ever had to give a speech? Did you try to convince others to see your side of something? How did you feel?

▶ On his flight to freedom, Frederick Douglass was protected by the Underground Railway network. Find out more about the Underground Railway.

4

Today is Newspaper Carrier Day in the United States. The first newsboy, 10-year-old Barney Flaherty, was hired on September 4, 1833.

▶ What is a newspaper? What does a newspaper carrier do?

▶ What kind of headline would you write for today's events in your classroom? your school?

▶ Does your local newspaper have carriers? If so, find out what their job involves and what they are paid.

Today is Be Late for Something Day. Sponsored by the Procrastinators' Club of America, the day is for people who have trouble being on time.

▶ What does it mean to be on time? What is a procrastinator? What is an antonym for late?

▶ Name an instance when you should never be late. When is it okay to be late?

▶ Find out what would happen if you were late doing the following: returning a library book, registering for school, paying a bill, signing up for a sports team

The Boston Bicycle Club sponsored the first 100-mile bike trip in America in 1882. Seven cyclists rode from Worcester, Massachusetts, to Boston in about 17 hours.

▶ Name things that you can ride. Classify the things into two groups: Powered by People and Powered by Something Else.

▶ Have you ever gone on a long bike ride? What are some problems that might occur on a long ride? How would you prepare for these problems?

▶ On a map find a location about 100 miles from where you live.

This is Grandma Moses Day. Grandma Moses was a famous painter. She never had an art lesson and didn't begin painting until she was 78. She was born on September 7, 1860.

▶ What tools do painters use?

▶ Grandma Moses first embroidered pictures on canvas. When the embroidery needles hurt her arthritic fingers, she started to paint. Compare embroidery and painting. How are they alike? How are they different?

▶ Look at examples of Grandma Moses's work. How would you describe her work?

On September 8, 1998, Mark McGwire hit his 62nd home run, breaking the record for most home runs in a single season. McGwire plays with the St. Louis Cardinals baseball team.

▶ What is a home run? What is a baseball season?

▶ A few days after Mark McGwire hit his record-breaking home run, Sammy Sosa of the Chicago Cubs hit his 62nd home run. How would you feel if you did something noteworthy just after someone else had done it?

▶ Find out what the current home run record is. Who holds the record?

Today the city of Ribeauvillé, France, celebrates the Day of the Flutes. Jugglers and troubadours join other musicians as they parade through the streets.

▶ What is a juggler? Name some things that you might juggle. What is a troubadour?

▶ The flute is a wind instrument, played when air is blown into it. Name other sounds that are made by blowing air.

▶ Choose a musical instrument and find out whether it is a wind instrument. Tell how sounds are made with the instrument.

After spending 19 years in captivity, on September 10, 1998, Keiko returned to his home in the waters off Iceland. Keiko is the killer whale who starred in the film *Free Willy*.

▶ What is captivity?

▶ Do you think animals should be used in making films? Explain why you think as you do.

▶ Choose a famous animal movie star. Find out about its movies and its life.

The nomadic camel herders in the desert of northern Niger in Africa celebrate Cure Salée on September 11. This festival is held in celebration of the first rains of the season.

▶ What is a herder? What does nomadic mean?

▶ Why would rain be cause for celebration for the herders? What other rain celebrations do you know about?

▶ Choose a weather-related holiday. Tell about the holiday and explain what type of weather is celebrated.

Today is Video Games Day.

▶ What is a video game?

▶ Have you ever played a video game? What is your favorite video game?

▶ Video games require some special equipment. List the equipment required to play a specific game. Explain what each piece of equipment does.

13

The Muppet Show premiered on television on September 13, 1976. Hosted by Kermit the Frog, the show was broadcast in more than 100 countries.

► The Muppets are puppets created by Jim Henson. Explain what a puppet is.

► Have you ever seen the Muppets? What make the Muppets unique puppets?

► Tell which Muppet character is your favorite. Describe how the character looks and what traits the character has.

14

Today is Star-Spangled Banner Day in the United States. In 1814 Francis Scott Key wrote "The Star-Spangled Banner," which became the national anthem in 1931.

► Define the following words from the anthem: dawn, hail, twilight, broad, perilous, rampart, gallantly

► Why would a country have a national anthem? Name places where you would hear or sing your national anthem.

► Learn more about the writing of "The Star Spangled Banner."

Today is Respect for the Aged Day in Japan. On this day Japan honors all of its elderly citizens.

▸ What does respect mean? Who are the aged?

▸ Would you want to live to be 100 years old? Why or why not?

▸ Find out about special programs for the elderly in your community. How can you show respect for the elderly?

Today is National Play-doh® Day in the United States. Joe McVicker of Cincinnati sent some nontoxic wallpaper cleaner to his sister-in-law, a nursery school teacher. She used it as a replacement for modeling clay.

▸ Describe dough. Do the words that you thought of also describe Play-doh?

▸ Have you ever played with Play-doh or modeling clay? Which do you prefer? Tell why.

▸ Make something using some kind of clay. Write step-by-step directions so that someone else could make the same thing.

Today is U.S. Citizenship Day. The United States Constitution was completed and signed on this day in 1787.

► What does the word citizen mean?

► All human beings are citizens of Earth, as well as their individual nations, states, cities, or towns. How can you be a good citizen of your school? your town? your country? the world?

► Find out how an immigrant to your country becomes a citizen.

On September 18, 1830, the first locomotive built in America, the *Tom Thumb*, lost a race with a horse. The steam engine had mechanical difficulties on the nine-mile course. A boiler leak prevented it from finishing the race.

► What is a locomotive? Why do you think they were nicknamed "iron horses"?

► Would you rather ride on a horse or a train? Explain why.

► Learn more about the history of railroads. Create a time line showing important events in their development.

In 1783 a hot-air balloon made a flight with passengers for the first time. The passengers were a sheep, a rooster, and a duck.

▶ What is a passenger? Give a synonym for the word.

▶ Imagine what the first passengers might have said as the balloon began its ascent. Do you think they enjoyed the flight? Tell why or why not.

▶ Find out how a hot-air balloon operates.

Indonesians participate in a Kite-Flying Competition today. Ten competitors launch their kites. As the lines cross, the kites break free and disappear into the sky. The winner is the person whose kite remains attached to its line.

▶ What is a competitor? Tell a way that you have competed with someone.

▶ In Indonesia the best competition kites are flown on lines coated with crushed glass. Why? What would you do to keep your kite string from being cut?

▶ Design a kite. What shape will it be?

21

Hurricane Hugo hit the American coastline near Charleston, South Carolina, on September 21, 1989. It left destruction totaling at least $8 billion.

▶ What is a hurricane? Where do they usually occur?

▶ Have you ever been in an area threatened by a hurricane? What can people do to protect themselves from a hurricane?

▶ Find out how hurricanes get their names.

22

September 22 is Elephant Appreciation Day. Wayne Hepburn, the founder of the day, says that elephants are examples of courage, strength, self-reliance, patience, and persistence.

▶ How would you describe an elephant? Make a list of all the words you could use.

▶ How would you show appreciation for something? Has anyone ever told you that they appreciated you? How did it make you feel?

▶ The first Elephant Appreciation Day was held in 1996. Think of a special appreciation day that you would like to begin. Write a paragraph explaining why the day should be held.

23

The planet Neptune was discovered on September 23, 1846, by German astronomer Johann Galle. Neptune is the eighth planet from the sun.

▶ What is an astronomer?

▶ How do you think Johann Galle made his discovery?

▶ There are nine planets in our solar system. List the names of all the planets in order. What other things make up the solar system?

24

September 24 is Heritage Day in South Africa. This public holiday recognizes and celebrates the diverse groups of people found within South Africa.

▶ What is diverse? What is a synonym for diverse?

▶ What diversity do you see in your classroom? your community? your nation?

▶ Learn more about the diversity of South Africa. Do all South Africans speak the same language? Do they live in the same type of community? Do they go to the same church?

In 1513 Vasco Núñez de Balboa discovered the Pacific Ocean. He stood high atop a peak in present-day Panama and looked out onto the ocean.

▶ What does the word pacific mean?

▶ Have you ever seen an ocean? How would you describe the ocean? Are there times when oceans change in appearance?

▶ Name all the oceans and describe their locations.

John Chapman was born on September 26, 1774. He is better known as Johnny Appleseed—planter of orchards and a friend of wild animals.

▶ What is an orchard? Why would orchards be helpful to settlers?

▶ Would you have liked to have known Johnny Appleseed? Tell why or why not.

▶ The tale of Johnny Appleseed is a story about a real man. Find another tale with a basis in history. Tell the tale and explain its truth.

Thomas Nast was born in 1840. Mr. Nast was a famous political cartoonist. His cartoons helped people to think about and understand important current events.

▶ What does a political cartoonist draw cartoons about?

▶ Mr. Nast created the cartoon symbols for the U.S. Democratic party (the donkey) and the Republican party (the elephant). How would you describe a donkey and an elephant? Have you ever seen these symbols used? What do the symbols say about how Mr. Nast might have felt about the two political parties?

▶ Find a political cartoon and tell about the current issues it is addressing.

In Taiwan, September 28 is a national holiday designated as Teachers' Day. The date was chosen because it is also the birthday of Confucius. Confucius spent 40 years as a teacher.

▶ Give several synonyms for the word teach.

▶ Confucius said that if you give a man a fish, you feed him for a day. But if you teach a man how to fish, you feed him for a lifetime. Do you agree? Tell why or why not.

▶ Many of the wise sayings of Confucius are remembered today. Find a list of these sayings. Choose one that you like. Make a sign or a bumper sticker using the words.

Happy Birthday to Stan Berenstain! He was born in Philadelphia, Pennsylvania, in 1923. He worked with his wife to create the Berenstain Bears books.

▶ The Berenstain Bears personify a human family. What does personify mean?

▶ The Berenstain books are written in rhyme. Do you like stories that are told in rhyme? Tell why or why not. Why do you think an author might use rhyme in a story?

▶ Many of the Berenstain books are filled with information and humor. Read one and list the facts you learned. Tell what you thought was funny.

On September 30, 1960, *The Flintstones* premiered on television. This cartoon comedy is about two Stone Age families—the Flintstones and the Rubbles.

▶ *The Flintstones* is set in prehistoric times. What does prehistoric mean?

▶ Fred Flintstone drives a car with stone wheels, and the family has a pet dinosaur. Could that happen? Why or why not? Give other similar examples.

▶ Think of a thing that you use every day. Pretend that the same thing existed in the Flintstones' household. Draw a picture of what it might look like.

Computer
Learning Month

Diversity
Awareness Month

International
Dinosaur Month

National Popcorn
Poppin' Month

October

What Happened Today? • EMC 1015

1

The first CD player went on sale on October 1, 1982. It was developed jointly by Sony, Philips, and Polygram. It cost $625 (over $1,000 in current dollars).

- ▶ CD is an abbreviation. What do the letters CD stand for?

- ▶ Do you have a CD player? What are CDs? How has the development of CD technology changed the way people listen to music?

- ▶ Find out what a CD player costs today. Is the price higher or lower than in 1982? Why?

2

The *Peanuts* comic strip created by Charles Schultz debuted on October 2, 1950. The strip featured Charlie Brown and his dog Snoopy.

- ▶ How would you describe Charlie Brown? Snoopy?

- ▶ What is your favorite comic strip? Why?

- ▶ If you were going to create your own comic strip, what would it be about? Draw a sample strip.

In 1990, after 45 years of being divided, East and West Germany were reunited. The new, united Germany took the name The Federal Republic of Germany.

▶ What is a synonym for divided?

▶ What are some reasons that an area might be divided? What problems might occur?

▶ Have other countries divided and then reunited? List the ones you discover.

On October 4, 1957, the first successful manmade earth satellite *Sputnik I* was launched. It weighed 184 pounds. This launch marked the beginning of our exploration beyond Earth.

▶ Tell the difference between a natural satellite and a manmade satellite. Can you name a natural satellite of Earth?

▶ Is 184 pounds huge? Find something that weighs about 184 pounds and imagine it orbiting Earth. Would you label *Sputnik I* as big or little? Tell why.

▶ Find out what *Sputnik I* did as it orbited Earth. Did it have a large effect on the future of space exploration?

Tecumseh, Shawnee chieftain and orator, died in battle in 1813. Tecumseh was an important Native American. He tried to organize an Indian confederation to stop white settlers from taking over Indian lands.

- ▶ Tecumseh advocated negotiation. What does advocated mean? What is negotiation?

- ▶ When Tecumseh visited tribes around the U.S., he condemned chieftains who had entered into agreements to give away their land. Do you think these agreements were right? Tell why or why not.

- ▶ Learn more about Tecumseh and his brother, Tenskwatawa.

In China, October 6 is the Festival of Chung Yeung. The festival remembers an old story of the Han Dynasty in which a soothsayer advised a man to take his family to a high place for 24 hours on the ninth day of the ninth moon. The man obeyed. When he returned home, he found that all living things had died. Chinese people climb to high places as a part of the celebration.

- ▶ Give a synonym for soothsayer.

- ▶ Tell about a time when you were given advice and followed it. Were you glad that you had?

- ▶ Choose another Chinese festival. Why is the festival held?

7

On October 7, 1983, Cabbage Patch Kids® were introduced. These dolls came with their own birth certificates and adoption papers.

- ▶ What does it mean to be adopted?

- ▶ Do you have a favorite doll or stuffed animal? Does your favorite have a name? Do you feel like you adopted it?

- ▶ What information is included on a birth certificate? When is a birth certificate used?

8

In 1871 the Great Chicago Fire began. According to legend, the fire was started when a cow kicked over a lantern in a barn filled with straw. The fire lasted for three days and destroyed 17,450 buildings.

- ▶ In the United States, the first or second week in October is Fire Prevention Week. What does the word prevention mean?

- ▶ What can you do to prevent fires from occurring? What should you do in case of a fire?

- ▶ Another disastrous fire occurred on the same day as the Great Chicago Fire—the Peshtigo Forest Fire. Find out more about this fire.

October 9 is Leif Eriksson* Day in Iceland and the United States. The day honors the Norse explorer who is believed to have been the first European to visit the American continent over 1,000 years ago.

▶ What is a continent? Name the seven continents. Tell which continent Leif Eriksson sailed from.

▶ Eriksson's ship was very different from Columbus's three ships. It had no below-deck storage areas and just one sail. How would the Vikingship voyage be different from Columbus's voyage?

▶ Gunnar Marel built a Vikingship of his own, the *Icelander.* He repeated Leif Eriksson's voyage of discovery. Find out more about this modern-day Viking.

*sometimes spelled Ericson

The tuxedo made its debut in New York in 1886.

▶ What is a tuxedo? Often the word tuxedo is shortened to tux. Give the longer form for these shortened words: auto, phone, fridge, gym.

▶ Have you ever used a shortened word? Tell what the word was and why you used it.

▶ List other words that are more commonly known by their shortened versions.

11

Eleanor Roosevelt was born on October 11, 1884. She was the wife of President Franklin Delano Roosevelt. An active and independent person, Mrs. Roosevelt was the first First Lady to give her own news conferences. When the United Nations was founded, she represented the United States as a delegate.

- ▶ What does the term First Lady mean? How do you think it came to be?

- ▶ Eleanor Roosevelt wrote "No one can make you feel inferior without your consent." What does this mean to you?

- ▶ Learn more about Eleanor Roosevelt. Find out why she was called "the first lady of the world."

12

October 12, 1999, is the Day of the Six Billion. According to the United Nations, the population of the world reached six billion on this date.

- ▶ What is population?

- ▶ In 1804 the world's population reached one billion. Today, a billion people are added to the population about every 12 years. Why does it take fewer years to add a billion new people than it used to take?

- ▶ Find the population of your city or town, your state or province, and your country.

The cornerstone of the White House was laid on October 13, 1792. The oldest building in Washington, D.C., the White House was first occupied by the family of President John Adams in November 1800.

▶ The White House is the presidential residence. What is a **residence**? Give some synonyms for residence.

▶ The White House has more than 100 rooms. What do you think it would be like to live in a house that big? Would you like to? Tell why or why not.

▶ Take a virtual tour of the White House or read more about the house at 1600 Pennsylvania Ave. NW.

On October 14, 1947, the sound barrier was broken. U.S. Air Force pilot Chuck Yeager flew faster than the speed of sound above Muroc Dry Lake Bed in California.

▶ What is a barrier? Give several synonyms for barrier.

▶ List things that go really fast. Are any of these things supersonic (faster than the speed of sound)?

▶ Chuck Yeager flew a *Bell X-1*. Find out more about this aircraft.

Bah humbug! It's National Grouch Day.

▶ Describe a grouch.

▶ What makes you grouchy? Explain.

▶ Think of a famous fictional character who was a grouch. Write a description of the character.

Today is Dictionary Day. Noah Webster, the American teacher and lexicographer who compiled the earliest dictionaries of the English language, was born on October 16, 1843.

▶ What is a lexicographer?

▶ Describe a dictionary. What different types of information are included in a dictionary?

▶ Find a word in your reading that you don't understand. Look it up in the dictionary. Use the word today as you talk and write.

October 17 is Black Poetry Day. The day commemorates the 1711 birth of Jupiter Hammon, the first published black poet in America. Jupiter Hammon was born into slavery but was taught to read and allowed to use his master's library.

▶ What does it mean to **publish** something? What kinds of things are published?

▶ Jupiter Hammon's first published poem was called "An Evening Thought." What ideas would you include in a poem with that title?

▶ Read poetry written by another African-American poet.

Shel Silverstein, children's cartoonist and poet, was born on October 18, 1932. Best known for his poetry books *A Light in the Attic*, *The Giving Tree*, and *Where the Sidewalk Ends*, he also wrote songs.

▶ What is an attic? The cartoon on the cover of *A Light in the Attic* shows a child with a light in his head. What comparison is Shel Silverstein making with this cartoon?

▶ Read several of Shel Silverstein's poems. What do you like best about his poetry?

▶ Shel Silverstein wrote "The Unicorn Song" and "A Boy Named Sue." Read the lyrics to these songs. Tell the morals of the stories.

October 19 is the day of Ebisu, one of the seven Japanese gods of luck. Japanese worshippers honor Ebisu with large white pickled radishes, *bettera*, bought at the pickle market.

▶ Describe a **pickle**. Tell how it looks, how it smells, how it tastes, and how it feels.

▶ Do you like pickles? Tell why or why not.

▶ Find out how pickles are made. Can pickles be made from different vegetables?

Happy Birthday to Crockett Johnson! Born in 1906, Johnson wrote *Harold and the Purple Crayon*. Crockett Johnson was a pseudonym. The author's real name was David Leisk.

▶ What is a **pseudonym**?

▶ Do you know any other authors that use a pseudonym? Why do you think someone might choose to use one?

▶ With his purple crayon, Harold drew one continuous line that became many different shapes. Try to draw something in your classroom using a continuous line.

Alfred Bernard Nobel, a Swedish chemist and engineer, was born on October 21, 1833. When he died in 1896, his will established the trust fund that supports the Nobel Prizes given every year since 1901.

▶ Give several synonyms for the word **prize**.

▶ Have you ever received a prize? What are prizes given for?

▶ What is a Nobel Prize? How are the prizes awarded?

Brian Boitano, Olympic gold medal figure skater was born in Mountain View, California, on October 22, 1963.

▶ What is a **figure skater**? Describe **ice skates**.

▶ Have you ever tried to walk on ice? to skate on ice? Tell about your experiences.

▶ When did Brian Boitano win his Olympic gold medal? Did he win additional honors?

Today is Chulalongkorn Day in Thailand. Flowers are laid at the foot of King Chulalongkorn's statue at the National Assembly Hall in Bangkok to celebrate the life of King Chulalongkorn the Great who died in 1910, after a 42-year reign. He abolished slavery in Thailand.

▶ What does it mean to **abolish** something?

▶ Putting flowers at the foot of a statue is a kind of tribute. Do you do something that is a tribute to someone or something? Tell about it.

▶ Locate Thailand on a globe. Find its capital, Bangkok. What kind of a government does Thailand have today?

On October 24, 1945, the United Nations was born. It was created to serve as an international peacekeeping organization. Today more than 155 nations send representatives to the UN's headquarters in New York City.

▶ What does **united** mean?

▶ An olive branch stands for peace. The UN flag shows the earth wreathed by olive branches. Do you think this is a good symbol for the United Nations? Tell why or why not.

▶ Learn more about the different organizations sponsored by the United Nations.

October 25

Pablo Ruiz Picasso was born on October 25, 1881. Picasso became one of the greatest artists of the twentieth century.

- ▶ What is a century? What century is it now?

- ▶ Picasso was a painter, a sculptor, and an engraver. What is your favorite art form? Tell why.

- ▶ Look at photographs of Picasso's work. Learn more about his style and what made him so famous.

October 26

Today is Mule Day. It is the anniversary of the delivery of the first mules to the United States. They were a gift from King Charles III of Spain.

- ▶ What is an anniversary?

- ▶ Do you think mules were a good gift to give a country? Tell why or why not.

- ▶ Learn more about mules and how they are used today.

On October 27, 1904, the New York City subway began operation with a 26-minute run from City Hall to West 145th Street. The new transit system was a hit—150,000 New Yorkers rode it that first day.

▸ What is a **subway**?

▸ What are the disadvantages and advantages of an underground transportation system?

▸ What mass transit is available in your area? Is it successful?

In 1886 Sculptor Frederic Auguste Bartholdi's Statue of Liberty was unveiled and dedicated in New York. The statue was named "Liberty Enlightening the World."

▸ What does **enlighten** mean?

▸ Do you think the name given to the statue is a good one? What would you name it? Tell why.

▸ What poem is carved on the base of the statue? Find a copy of the poem and read it.

159

On October 29, 1969, data flowed between a computer at UCLA and a computer at the Stanford Research Institute. This was the beginning of the Internet as we know it.

▶ What is **data**? Give a synonym for data.

▶ What can you do on the Internet? Do you think the Internet is helpful to you? to businesses?

▶ Use a search engine and your computer to learn more about the history of the Internet.

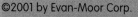

Happy Birthday, Emily Post! Born in 1872, Emily Post is remembered for her book on manners and etiquette, first published in 1922.

▶ What are **manners**? What is **etiquette**?

▶ Do you think that good manners are important? Which manners do you consider most important?

▶ Emily Post gave advice for manners in specific situations. Her granddaughter still writes a column today. Locate an article or column and read about good manners and proper behavior.

31

Harry Houdini died on October 31, 1926. Houdini was one of the world's greatest magicians. The anniversary of his death is observed as National Magic Day in the United States.

▶ What is a magician?

▶ Have you ever performed a magic trick? Tell about it.

▶ Harry Houdini was famous for his death-defying escapes. Learn more about these escapes.

Aviation History Month

International Drum Month

National American Indian Heritage Month

Peanut Butter Lovers' Month

November

Today is National Author's Day in the United States. It was first celebrated in 1929.

▶ An author could write about many different things. List as many as you can.

▶ Who is your favorite author? Why?

▶ If you were going to write a book, what would it be about? Who would your characters be? What would they be like?

Happy Birthday, Daniel Boone! An American frontiersman, explorer, and militia officer, Daniel Boone was born on November 2, 1734.

▶ What is a frontiersman?

▶ Would you like the rugged life of an explorer and frontiersman? Tell why or why not.

▶ In 1778 Daniel Boone was captured by Shawnee Indians. Chief Blackfish adopted him and named him "Big Turtle." Find out about another of Daniel Boone's captures.

John Montague, the Earl of Sandwich, was born in 1718. Legend has it that the Earl loved to play cards and didn't like to stop to eat. One time, in the middle of a long game, he got hungry and ordered a piece of meat between two slices of bread. Ta-dah—the first sandwich!

▶ Make a list of different kinds of sandwiches. Divide the list into categories.

▶ What is your favorite sandwich? Describe how to make it step by step.

▶ Find a recipe for a new kind of sandwich. Try it out!

On November 4, 1922, one of the most important archaeological discoveries of modern times occurred at Luxor, Egypt. English archaeologist Howard Carter discovered the tomb of Egypt's child-king, Tutankhamen.

▶ What is an archaeologist? What is a tomb?

▶ Tutankhamen became pharaoh of Egypt when he was nine. Do you think a nine-year-old can rule a country? Tell why or why not.

▶ Learn more about the treasures recovered from King Tut's tomb.

Roy Rogers, the King of the Cowboys, was born in 1912. He was famous for his cowboy songs and cowboy movies.

▶ How would you describe a cowboy?

▶ Roy Rogers' theme song was "Happy Trails to You." What song would you like to have as your theme song?

▶ Learn more about Roy Rogers and his horse Trigger.

November 6 is Saxophone Day. In 1814 Adolphe Sax was born in Belgium. His father was a musical instrument maker. When Adolphe grew up he became a musician and invented the saxophone.

▶ What does the suffix -phone mean? Why do you think Adolphe Sax named his new instrument the "saxophone"?

▶ If you were to invent a musical instrument, what would it be like?

▶ There are many different kinds of saxophones. Find out more about the saxophone family.

Marie Sklodowska Curie was born on November 7, 1867, in Warsaw, Poland. She became a famous chemist and physicist. In 1903 she and her husband Pierre were awarded the Nobel Prize in physics. They had discovered the element radium, which led to the development of the x-ray process. She won the Nobel Prize in chemistry in 1911.

▶ What does a chemist do? What is an element?

▶ Madam Curie was one of the first women scientists to be recognized in her field. Why do you think that historically more men were noted scientists?

▶ Learn more about Madam Curie's life.

Edmund Halley was born on November 8, 1656. As the Royal Astronomer he observed the great comet of 1682 and predicted that it would return in 1758. It did, and the comet was named for him. The most recent appearance of comet Halley was in 1986.

▶ What is a comet?

▶ There have been 28 recorded appearances of comet Halley since 240 B.C. The average time between appearances is 76 years. Predict its next few appearances.

▶ Choose another comet. Learn about its path and how often it is observed from Earth.

Happy Birthday, Benjamin Banneker! Benjamin Banneker was born on November 9, 1731. He taught himself astronomy and higher mathematics, wrote an almanac, and carved wooden clockworks. He is remembered as the first black man of science.

▶ What are clockworks? What other names might you use to describe them?

▶ List some of the many different kinds of scientists. What kind of a scientist would you like to be? Tell why.

▶ Benjamin Banneker built the first clock that was made completely in America. How were the clocks in the eighteenth century different from those of the twenty-first century?

The television program *Sesame Street* debuted on November 10, 1969. The setting of the popular television show is a city street. People and puppets who live along the street teach young children their letters, numbers, and other lessons.

▶ What is a setting?

▶ What is your favorite television program? Describe its setting.

▶ Choose a *Sesame Street* character. Describe the character and its function on the television show.

Today is Veterans Day in the United States. Americans remember and honor soldiers of all wars. Veterans Day commemorates the day the armistice, or peace agreement, was signed, ending World War I in 1918.

▶ What is a veteran?

▶ What does your community do to honor and remember its veterans? Do you participate in any of these events?

▶ Find out more about the signing of the World War I armistice.

Every fall the new Lord Mayor of London takes office in a series of civic ceremonies that culminate with the Lord Mayor's Show on or near November 12. (The official date is the second Saturday in November.) The Lord Mayor, dressed in a scarlet gown, rides through the city in a gilded coach drawn by six matched horses.

▶ The word coach has several meanings. Give as many as you can.

▶ What would it feel like to ride through the streets in a gilded coach? Would you like to do it? Why or why not?

▶ Who is the current Lord Mayor of London? What does the Lord Mayor do?

Happy Birthday, Robert Louis Stevenson! Born on November 13, 1850, in Edinburgh, Scotland, Robert Louis Stevenson was a famous author of adventure stories. He once drew a treasure map for his stepson and then wrote a book about the map. The book was called *Treasure Island*.

▶ What is an adventure? List some outings you would consider adventures.

▶ What makes an adventure story different from a biography? Do you like adventure stories? Why or why not?

▶ Read part of *Treasure Island*. Describe the island.

On November 14, 1889, newspaper reporter Nellie Bly set off to travel around the world. Author Jules Verne had just written a book about Phileas Fogg, an imaginary character who traveled around the world in 80 days. Nellie Bly wanted to beat that record.

▶ Phileas Fogg's record was imaginary. What would Nellie Bly's record be?

▶ Nellie Bly did break the record. She completed her trip in just over 72 days. Do you think you could make the trip that quickly? Tell why or why not.

▶ The route that someone travels is called his or her itinerary. Plan an itinerary for a trip around the world.

In Japan, families celebrate Shichi-Go-San on November 15 of each year. Parents take their three-year-old children, five-year-old boys, and seven-year-old girls to their local parish, where they give thanks for the children's healthy growth.

▶ The children often dress in traditional kimonos for the ceremony. What is a kimono?

▶ Do you celebrate any holiday that requires you to be a specific age? Tell about it.

▶ Why is this celebration called Shichi-Go-San? Hint: Counting in Japanese will help you answer the question.

The United Nations designated today as the International Day for Tolerance.

▶ What is tolerance?

▶ How can you show tolerance for others?

▶ Review your school rules or code of conduct. Tell which parts encourage tolerance.

Every year on November 17, people in Thailand celebrate Loy Krathong, the Festival of the Floating Leaf Cups. They make little leaf boats, krathong, out of lotus or banana leaves. After dark, they light candles, put them in the boats, set the boats afloat, and watch them float away.

▶ The leaf boats float on the river. What other words describe movement in water or air?

▶ The Thai people believe that if you make a wish and your candle stays lit until the krathong disappears, the wish will come true. Do you agree? What is a name you might use for this kind of a belief?

▶ Choose a superstition and explain it.

Louis Jacques Mande Deguerre was born on November 18, 1789. He is remembered for his invention of the daguerreotype—a process that produced an image on a plate of silver or silver-covered copper.

▶ What is an image?

▶ Why do families like to have photographs? Do you have family photos? Where do you keep them?

▶ The daguerreotype process took 20 to 30 minutes. Find out more about the process used to develop photos today.

U.S. President Lincoln delivered his famous Gettysburg Address in 1863. He was taking part in the dedication of a national cemetery on the site of a Civil War battlefield. His speech began, "Four score and seven years ago...."

▶ How many years are in a score? How long is four score and seven years?

▶ President Lincoln delivered his address in less than two minutes. What other words might you use instead of saying delivered his address?

▶ Read the Gettysburg Address. Do Lincoln's ideas seem important to you today? Tell why or why not.

It's Universal Children's Day. On November 20, 1959, the United Nations General Assembly adopted the Declaration of the Rights of the Child. This anniversary is celebrated by 120 different countries.

▶ What is a declaration? What are rights?

▶ Do you have certain rights? What rights do all children have?

▶ Read the U.N. Declaration of the Rights of the Child.

Hello! Today is World Hello Day. Participate by greeting 10 people today.

▶ List phrases and words that you use when you greet someone.

▶ Besides your family and classmates, what 10 people could you say "Hello" to today?

▶ World Hello Day has been celebrated since 1973. Find out more about the history of the day by contacting The McCormack Brothers, Box 993, Omaha, NE 68101 (www.worldhelloday.org).

In the United States today is National Stop the Violence Day. Radio and television stations across the nation are encouraged to promote peace on the streets. The observation marks the anniversary of President John F. Kennedy's assassination.

▶ What is an assassination?

▶ What can you do to stop violence and promote peace on the streets?

▶ Locate an organization in your community that works to stop violence.

November
24

John Lee Love patented the pencil sharpener in 1897. The Love sharpener was a simple, portable one. The pencil was inserted in the opening of the sharpener and rotated by hand. The shavings stayed inside the sharpener.

▶ Name things that need to be sharpened. Sort your list to show which things are sharpened to a point and which things are sharpened along an edge.

▶ How might you sharpen a pencil if you have no pencil sharpener?

▶ If you were going to invent a new pencil sharpener, what features would you want it to have?

Carlo Lorenzini was born in Italy on November 24, 1926. He called himself Carlo Collodi. He is remembered for his book *The Adventures of Pinocchio*.

▶ Pinocchio was a marionette. What is a marionette? How is a marionette different from a puppet?

▶ Pinocchio could laugh and dance even though he was carved out of wood. Choose a wooden thing. Tell about what would happen if it started laughing and dancing.

▶ Try making a puppet or a marionette. Can you make your puppet laugh and dance?

 What Happened Today? • EMC 1015

25

Happy Birthday, Joe DiMaggio! Joseph Paul DiMaggio was born on November 25, 1914. He is a Baseball Hall of Fame outfielder. In 1941 he got a hit in 56 consecutive games.

▸ What does it mean to get a hit? What does consecutive mean?

▸ Have you ever played baseball? What is your favorite position?

▸ List the nine positions played by the members of a baseball team. Tell about the job of each player.

26

On November 26, 1946, the Slinky® was introduced. Its inventor, Richard James, a naval engineer, was conducting an experiment with tension springs. During the experiment, one of the springs fell to the floor and began to "walk." He then got the idea for the toy.

▸ What is a spring?

▸ Do you think "Slinky" is a good name for a spring that "walks"? Why or why not?

▸ Choose another toy. Find out how it got its name. Tell whether you think it's a good name.

Happy Birthday, Kevin Henkes! Born on November 27, 1960, Kevin Henkes is an author and illustrator. He uses mice as characters in stories about important childhood dilemmas.

▶ What is a dilemma?

▶ Think of a dilemma that you have faced. Describe how you felt and what you did.

▶ Read one of Kevin Henkes' books. Tell about the character's dilemma.

Captain Cyril Turner of the Royal Air Force surprised the people of New York City on November 28, 1922, when he wrote in the sky! The white trail from his airplane spelled "Hello USA."

▶ Skywriting is a compound word invented to describe something. Name other compound words that begin with sky.

▶ What message would you like to write in the sky?

▶ Find out how pilots in airplanes leave messages in the sky.

Happy Birthday, Louisa May Alcott! Born in 1832 in Philadelphia, Pennsylvania, Louisa May Alcott wrote a story about a family of four girls growing up during the Civil War—*Little Women*. It was the story of her own family.

▶ *Little Women* is a classic story. What is a classic?

▶ Have you ever read *Little Women* or *Little Men*? Who was your favorite character?

▶ Find out more about Louisa May Alcott. Her success as an author allowed her to support her family.

Mark Twain was born on November 30, 1835. His real name was Samuel Langhorne Clemens. He was born in Florida, Missouri. He is best remembered for his books *The Adventures of Tom Sawyer* and *The Adventures of Huckleberry Finn*.

▶ One of Mr. Twain's other popular books is *The Prince and the Pauper*. What is a pauper?

▶ Mark Twain once said, "It is better to keep your mouth shut and appear stupid than to open it and remove all doubt." What do you think Mr. Twain meant?

▶ Find out more about Samuel Clemens' life.

Safe Toys and Gifts Month

Universal Human Rights Month

Tell Someone They're Doing a Good Job Week
(December 17-23)

Hanukkah
(eight days beginning on the 25th of the Hebrew month of Kislev)

December

What Happened Today? • EMC 1015

Today is Rosa Parks Day. On December 1, 1955, Ms. Parks was arrested in Alabama when she refused to give up her bus seat to a white man. Her act prompted a bus boycott led by Dr. Martin Luther King, Jr., and resulted in the desegregation of the bus system.

▶ What adjectives would you use to describe Ms. Parks?

▶ Do you think Rosa Parks was courageous? Why? How do you think she might have felt on the bus that day?

▶ Find out more about Rosa Parks.

On December 2, 1949, the song "Rudolph the Red-Nosed Reindeer" made its debut on the record charts.

▶ The name of the song is an example of alliteration— Rudolph the Red-Nosed Reindeer. Create another alliterative character name.

▶ What was Rudolph's problem? How was the problem solved?

▶ Explain the phrase "He turned a liability into an asset." Tell how the phrase applies to Rudolph's story.

The United Nations designated December 3 as an annual observance—International Day of Disabled Persons. The purpose of this day is to emphasize the need to make participation in everyday life accessible to people with disabilities.

▶ What does disabilities mean?

▶ What can be done to help a person in a wheelchair get into a public building? What can be done to help a blind person enter and ride an elevator?

▶ Find out how your community supports people with disabilities. How does your school show support?

On December 4, 1998, the U.S. space shuttle *Endeavour* took a component of the space station into orbit. Spacewalking astronauts fastened it to another component already in orbit. It will take a total of 45 U.S. and Russian launches to complete the space station by 2004.

▶ What is a component?

▶ Have you ever built a structure out of Legos® or Construx®? How was it like constructing the space station? What special problems do the astronauts face?

▶ Find out more about the International Space Station.

Happy Birthday, Walt Disney! Born on December 5, 1901, Walt Disney is an important person in the history of animated cartoons. When he won the Oscar for *Snow White and the Seven Dwarfs*, he received one big Oscar and seven little ones.

▶ What does animated mean?

▶ Mr. Disney is remembered for many movies and television shows, as well as cartoons. Tell about your favorite Disney character.

▶ Find out more about Walt Disney's life.

December 6 is St. Nicholas Day. St. Nicholas was a real bishop. In many European countries, children still celebrate the Feast Day of St. Nicholas. Some children leave hay and carrots in their shoes for St. Nicholas's horse. If they have been good, St. Nicholas fills their shoes with candies and presents in the night.

▶ Leaving carrots for St. Nicholas's horse is a custom. What is a custom?

▶ Dutch children leave carrots and hay in their shoes for St. Nicholas's horse. Do you have a similar custom? Tell about it.

▶ Find Europe on a world map. List the European countries.

On December 7, 1787, Delaware became the first state to ratify the proposed U.S. Constitution.

▸ What does it mean to ratify something?

▸ Have you ever helped to establish rules or procedures for a group? How did you resolve differences? Was your vote unanimous?

▸ Name the other 12 original states.

On December 8, 1991, the republics of Russia, Belarus, and Ukraine signed an agreement at Minsk, creating the Commonwealth of Independent States. This agreement formally began the breakup of the Union of Soviet Socialist Republics (the Soviet Union).

▸ Russia, Belarus, and the Ukraine formed an alliance. What is an alliance?

▸ If you were going to form an alliance with another person, what would you want to have in common with them? Is it important for different countries forming alliances to have things in common?

▸ Find out some of the ways the people and the land of the former Soviet Union were diverse. Do you think this diversity led to the breakup of the Soviet Union? Tell why or why not.

December 9

On December 9, 1848, American author Joel Chandler Harris was born in Eatonton, Georgia. Mr. Harris was the creator of the Uncle Remus stories.

▶ The Uncle Remus stories are a collection of tales about Brer Rabbit, Brer Bear, and Brer Fox. The tales are told in dialect. Joel Chandler Harris was one of the first authors to use dialect in his writing. What is dialect?

▶ Brer Rabbit often played tricks on the other characters. Name other tricksters that you have encountered in your reading. Tell about a trick they played.

▶ Try reading some of Harris's stories aloud.

December 10

December 10 is Human Rights Day in the United States. Begun by presidential proclamation in 1949, the day recognizes and celebrates the basic rights of every individual.

▶ What is the difference between a right and a privilege?

▶ December 10 is Human Rights Day. Do animals have basic rights too? Tell why or why not.

▶ Read the U.S. Bill of Rights and see what rights the U.S. government recognizes.

Sighting of the northern lights was first recorded in America on December 11, 1719. These lights are rays of color that appear in the sky like a huge curtain or pattern of smoke.

▶ Another name for the northern lights is the aurora borealis.
What is an aurora?

▶ The northern lights appear in the night sky. Have you seen the northern lights? What other lights have you seen in the night sky?

▶ Find out what causes the northern lights.

Today is Poinsettia Day. American diplomat Joel Roberts Poinsett died on December 12, 1851. He first brought the poinsettia plant into the United States from Mexico.

▶ Describe a poinsettia plant.

▶ The poinsettia has become a favorite winter-blooming houseplant. List plants that are houseplants and plants that grow outdoors. Are there some plants that grow in both environments?

▶ A plant that originates in a certain area is called a native. Choose a plant and find out if it is native to your area.

The Susan B. Anthony dollar was first minted on December 13, 1978. This was the first U.S. coin that honored a woman.

▶ What does minted mean?

▶ If you could select a woman to be honored on a coin, who would you pick? Why?

▶ Another dollar coin was minted in 2000. Which woman from American history does it honor?

In 1911 Roald Amundsen, along with 4 companions and 52 sled dogs, located and visited the South Pole.

▶ What is the South Pole? Show on a globe where it is located.

▶ What special problems would an expedition to the South Pole encounter? How could explorers prepare for these problems?

▶ Read an account of Amundsen's 1911 expedition. Then read about Captain Robert Scott's 1912 trip. Compare the two.

Happy Birthday, Alexandre Gustave Eiffel! Born on December 15, 1832, Eiffel designed the Eiffel Tower. The tower was built for the Paris International Exposition of 1889.

▶ What is a tower?

▶ The Eiffel Tower weighs more than 7,000 tons and is over 1,000 feet tall. It is made of wrought iron. What problems might be encountered constructing such a structure?

▶ Find a photograph of the Eiffel Tower. Write a short description of it.

Today is the anniversary of the Boston Tea Party in 1773. American patriots dumped 350 chests of tea into the harbor to protest a British tax on tea.

▶ What is a protest?

▶ Do you think taxes are a good idea? Why or why not? What kinds of taxes do we have to pay today?

▶ What was the result of the Boston Tea Party?

On December 17, 1790, the Aztec Calendar Stone was found beneath the ground by workmen repairing Mexico City's Central Plaza. The intricately carved stone records a 52-year cycle of the sun's movement.

▶ Describe a calendar.

▶ The Aztec Calendar Stone was carved in basalt. It is over 11 feet in diameter and weighs nearly 25 tons. What would be the disadvantages and advantages of having a calendar like that?

▶ Learn more about the Aztec civilization.

Steven Spielberg was born on December 18, 1947. As a child, he charged admission to his home movie productions, and his sister sold popcorn. Today he is known as "Mr. Show-Biz" and he is responsible for *E.T.: The Extra Terrestrial*, the *Indiana Jones* movies, and *Jurassic Park*. His movie *Schindler's List* won the Academy Award for best picture in 1993.

▶ Steven Spielberg is a writer, a producer, and a director. What is the difference among the jobs?

▶ What is your favorite movie? Tell why.

▶ Learn more about Steven Spielberg's life.

On December 19, 1958, the U.S. satellite *Atlas* transmitted the first voice radio broadcast from space. It was a 58-word recorded greeting from President Dwight D. Eisenhower.

▸ What does broadcast mean?

▸ If you could broadcast a greeting to all human beings, what would you want to say?

▸ Record a greeting from your class to another class or to your school and arrange to have it broadcast.

On December 20, 1803, one of the greatest real estate deals in history took place. More than a million square miles of land was turned over to the U.S. by France in the Louisiana Purchase.

▸ What is a purchase?

▸ The U.S. paid about $20 per square mile for its new land. About how much did it cost? Do you think the U.S. made a good purchase?

▸ The Louisiana Purchase nearly doubled the size of the U.S. Find maps to show the U.S. before and after the purchase.

What Happened Today? • EMC 1015

The first crossword puzzle was created by Arthur Wayne on December 21, 1913. It was published in the *New York World*.

► Describe a crossword puzzle.

► Do you like to work crossword puzzles? Tell why or why not.

► Create a crossword puzzle.

On December 22, 1956, the first gorilla was born in captivity. Colo was born at the Columbus, Ohio, zoo. The baby gorilla weighed a little over three pounds.

► What does captivity mean?

► Do you think that zoos are a good way to view animals? Tell why or why not?

► Learn more about gorillas and their natural habitat.

In Oaxaca, Mexico, it's the Night of the Radishes. Figures of people and animals are carved out of radishes and displayed in the city's annual radish sculpture competition.

▶ What is a competition?

▶ What difficulties would carving a radish pose? What advantages?

▶ The radishes grown in the country near Oaxaca are large, sometimes the length of a child's arm. Make a giant clay radish, and then sculpt a person or thing in the clay.

Happy Birthday, Kit Carson! Christopher Carson was born on December 24, 1809. He was a famous American frontiersman, soldier, trapper, and guide.

▶ What is a trapper?

▶ Trapping was important in the early 1800. Is trapping still done today? Do you think trapping is a good idea? Tell why or why not.

▶ Find out about trapping regulations in your community.

December 25

Merry Christmas! Christmas is the important Christian observance of the birth of Jesus of Nazareth. This day of caroling and gift giving is celebrated in many parts of the world.

▶ What is a synonym for merry?

▶ Do you celebrate Christmas? What kind of things do you do? If not, do you celebrate another winter holiday?

▶ Choose a country. Find out if Christmas is celebrated in that country.

December 26

December 26 is Boxing Day in Canada, the United Kingdom, and many other countries. Gifts are "boxed up" for public servants.

▶ What is a public servant?

▶ Do you think giving gifts to public servants is a good idea? Tell why or why not.

▶ Write a note to someone who serves you. Put it in a tiny box, wrap it up, and deliver it.

Chemist Louis Pasteur was born on December 27, 1822, in France. He is responsible for discovering the pasteurization process for milk.

▶ What does the word pasteurize mean?

▶ List the things you eat or drink that are made from milk.

▶ Find out more about the process of pasteurization.

William Finley Semple of Mount Vernon, Ohio, obtained the first chewing gum patent on December 28, 1869. His patent claimed the combination of rubber with other ingredients to form chewing gum. However, his recipe for chewing gum was never used commercially.

▶ What does the word commercially mean?

▶ Also in 1869, Thomas Adams tried to make a rubber substitute using chicle imported from Mexico. Instead of rubber, he made chewing gum. Have you ever started with one goal in mind and changed the goal midway through? Tell about your experience.

▶ Learn more about the history of chewing gum.

Happy Birthday, Molly Garrett Bang! Children's author and illustrator Molly Garrett Bang was born on December 29, 1943. A Caldecott Honor Award winner, she uses exquisite paintings and mixed media collages to tell important stories.

▸ Paint is one media and clay is another. What do you think mixed media means?

▸ In *Tye May and the Magic Brush,* an orphan girl teaches herself to paint so well that her paintings become real. She uses the paintbrush to help other poor people and to defend herself. Is Tye May like another heroine or hero? How are they similar? Different?

▸ Read several of Molly Garrett Bang's books. Tell about her style and her message.

Rudyard Kipling was born in Bombay, India, on December 30, 1865. He was a famous English poet and short story writer. He is best known for his children's stories like those in *The Jungle Book.* He won the Nobel Prize in literature.

▸ Rudyard Kipling worked as a journalist in India. What is a journalist?

▸ *The Jungle Book* describes an Indian boy named Mowgli who's brought up by wolves and becomes master of the jungle. Would it be possible for animals to raise a human? Tell why or why not.

▸ Read one of Rudyard Kipling's books or stories.

What Happened Today? • EMC 1015